"MY LIFE"

An emotional journey expressed in abstract paintings

Narrative and Paintings by: Une Oak Lee-Johnson

Published by: Ulee Press

First paperback edition February 2024

Book design by Une Oak Lee-Johnson

ISBN 979-8-9884566-0-5 (Hard Cover)

ISBN 979-8-9884566-2-9 (Paperback)

https://ulee.us/

Dedicated to Peter, who is always my helpful and loving husband.

Introduction

This book "My Life" is a series of paintings, generally one painting per year and in some cases more than one for a particularly significant year.

In my life I have gone through handicap, major depression after pregnancy and divorce. Being a sensitive artist these events significantly affected me. I overcame all these challenges to make and enjoy a happy and fulfilled life. Throughout my life I have always been committed to developing my art and it is this art that I use to create this book.

I studied German language and literature in Korea and interior architecture in New York and Paris France. The literature inspired me to write a book. I did not know what the content would be but I was determined to write a book later in life about My Life. After almost 50 years I felt ready to write. My life has been interesting and diverse, so I decided to combine my love for painting with my ambition to write a book. The concept is to highlight each year with a painting and a short description text.

The early years show the effect of the Korean war in 1953, the year I was born. The war was followed by my emotional conflict with my parents, the excitement of developing into an adult and all the freedoms and responsibilities of being an adult.

In the middle years, I went through some difficult times and major depression. These were the most challenging images to paint. It was emotionally draining to express my feelings and generate art for these years. The process of creating these paintings resurfaced the memories of those times. I was fearful that people would be critical of me and maybe avoid me, thinking I was unstable or even dangerous. Mental illness carries many misconceptions in people's minds. With the help of trusted friends and family, I eventually gained the confidence to open up about these events. I gained the strength to face those times honestly and hopefully help others suffering the same type of illness to have confidence and use the experience as a positive influence in their life.

The later years show my recovery and enjoyment of life and the adventures. I concentrated on painting. I won prestigious awards in New York City that gave me the confidence to paint what inspired me. My husband and I sailed our sailboat from New York City to the Caribbean. That adventure provided many inspirational ideas to develop my art. We renovated properties damaged by Hurricane Maria in Puerto Rico. We bought a neglected property in a hilltop medieval town in Italy and renovated that into a wonderful home. Life is now full of hope, adventure, and joy.

This book was written while I am alive and covers years 1 through 68 in the year 2022. I stopped there to publish the book. I hope to continue developing by living life and creating new art. I may add new paintings in a future update. I have no plans to do so now. Producing the paintings and writing about periods in my life has been very therapeutic. I am now ready to move on to other ideas. Please look at my website and Instagram page for my current ideas.

I enjoy hearing from my readers, please contact me with any thoughts and comments.

Acknowledgments

Producing an art book like this requires a lot of support and I want to thank those that helped me.

For translation to Korean and additional commentary on the paintings, I thank Sam-Huan Ahn. Sam reviewed the book helped with inspiration and added independent insights to each painting. He helped me get it published in Korea.

My husband Peter helped with all the computer work, photography, and printing. He needed much patience to cope with my frustrations and demands and he supported me all the way. Thank you Peter.

My family reviewed the book and gave me encouragement when I needed it. Thanks to all members of my family.

Chapter 1 – Handicapped and the war

I was born with one eye not developed. One eye was closed all the time and misshapen. I could only see through the one good eye. As a baby my face was disfigured and that affected the way other people reacted to me.

Because my bones were still developing I could not have corrective surgery until I was 11 years old. So my early years were a source of shame and stress for my mother. Korea at that time was a society that shunned handicap and disfigurement.

My mother thought she had done something wrong and was punished by having a handicapped baby. This is sadly untrue. I was growing inside my mother during a very stressful time at the end of the Korean War. She was malnourished and had to walk long distances to escape from the fighting and turmoil of the war. It is almost certain that this stress caused my disfigurement. Rather than sympathy and support there was always an undercurrent of blame and shame.

Although this time was hard for my mother I developed an independent spirit and personality. I had to stand up for myself at school. The first days at school were especially difficult for my mother as she had to take me to school and interact with all the other parents.

The paintings in this chapter cover years 1 through 10 and show my mother's stress and the conflicts I had with my Mother.

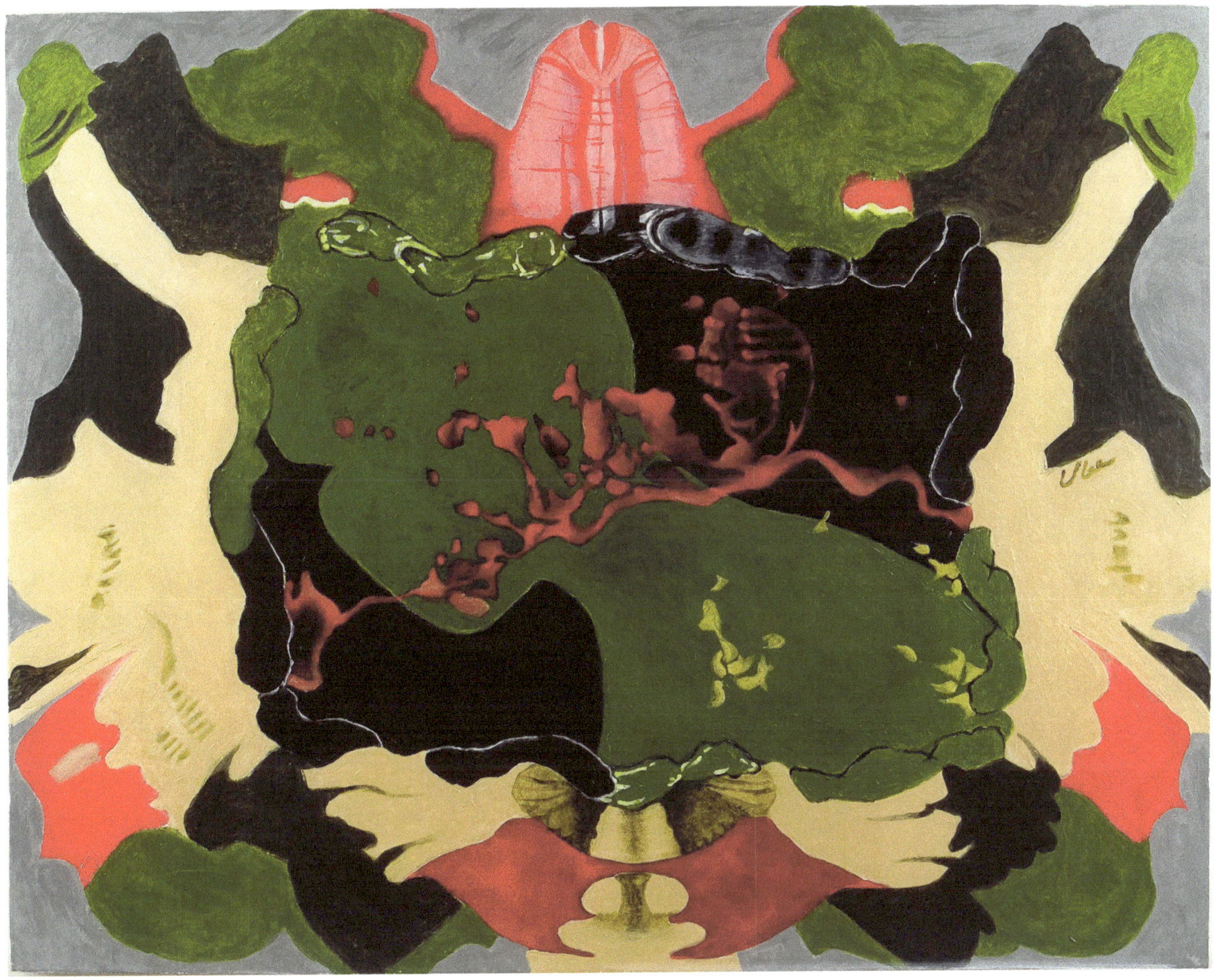

1 Year Old, Handicapped Baby

I was born handicapped. One of my eyes was not developed as normal and did not function. My mother thought she had done something wrong in having a handicapped baby. It was quite visible, one eye did not open at all. I was born during the last year of the Korean war. My mother was very depressed and stressed while I was developing inside her. My portrait in this painting shows that the handicap was not a big feature for me at all. My babyhood was influenced a lot by my mother's stress.

Acrylic on Canvas 40x30 inch

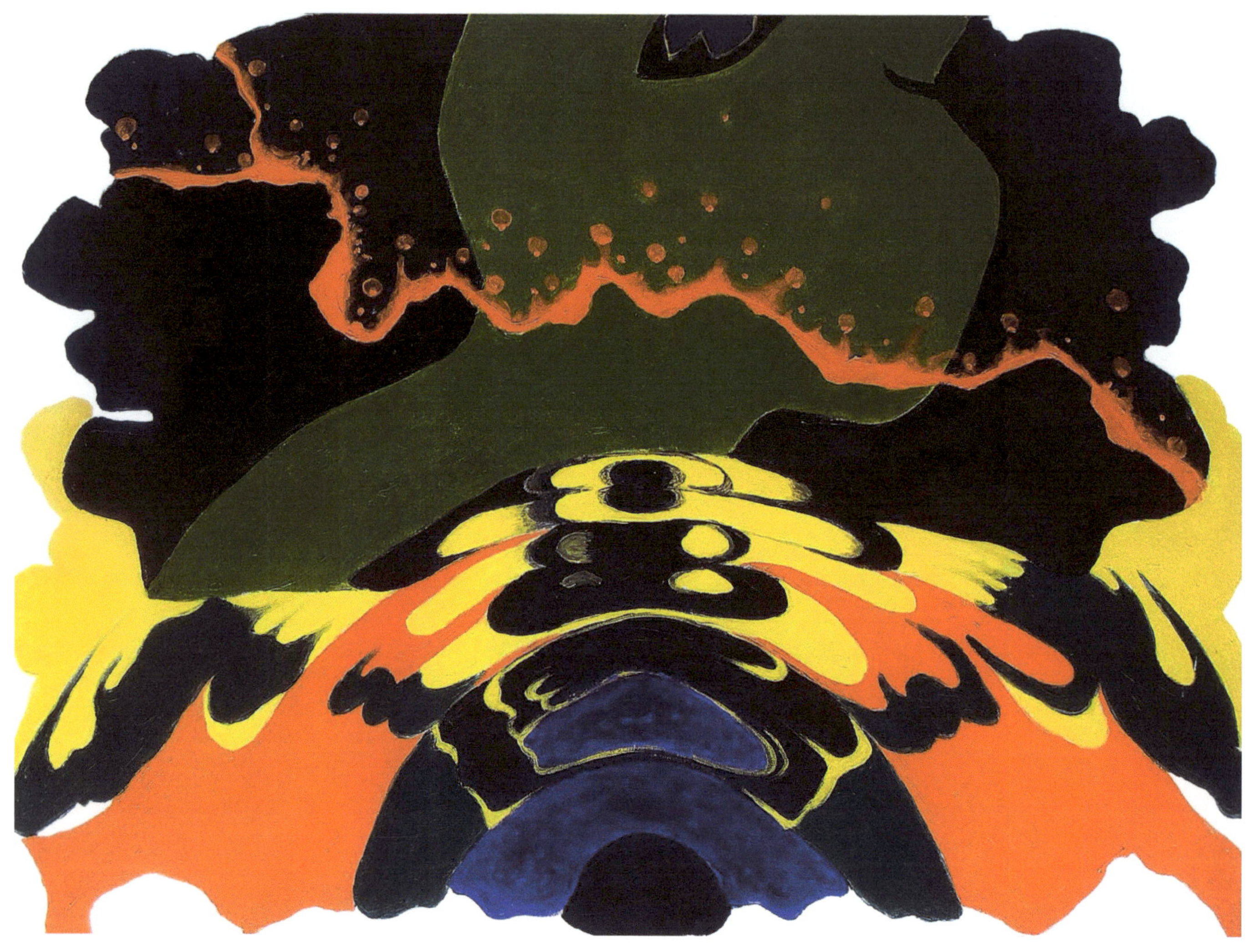

2 Years Old, The War

It was during my mother's refugee time. She did not know my father's whereabouts during the confusion of war. She was depressed to be alone feeling the effects of war and my handicap. My one eye was closed all the time. My mother was ashamed and did not have a desire to show me to the people. This painting shows one closed eye but I was not depressed at all. My mother said I was a really bright and energetic baby.

Acrylic on Canvas 40x30 inch

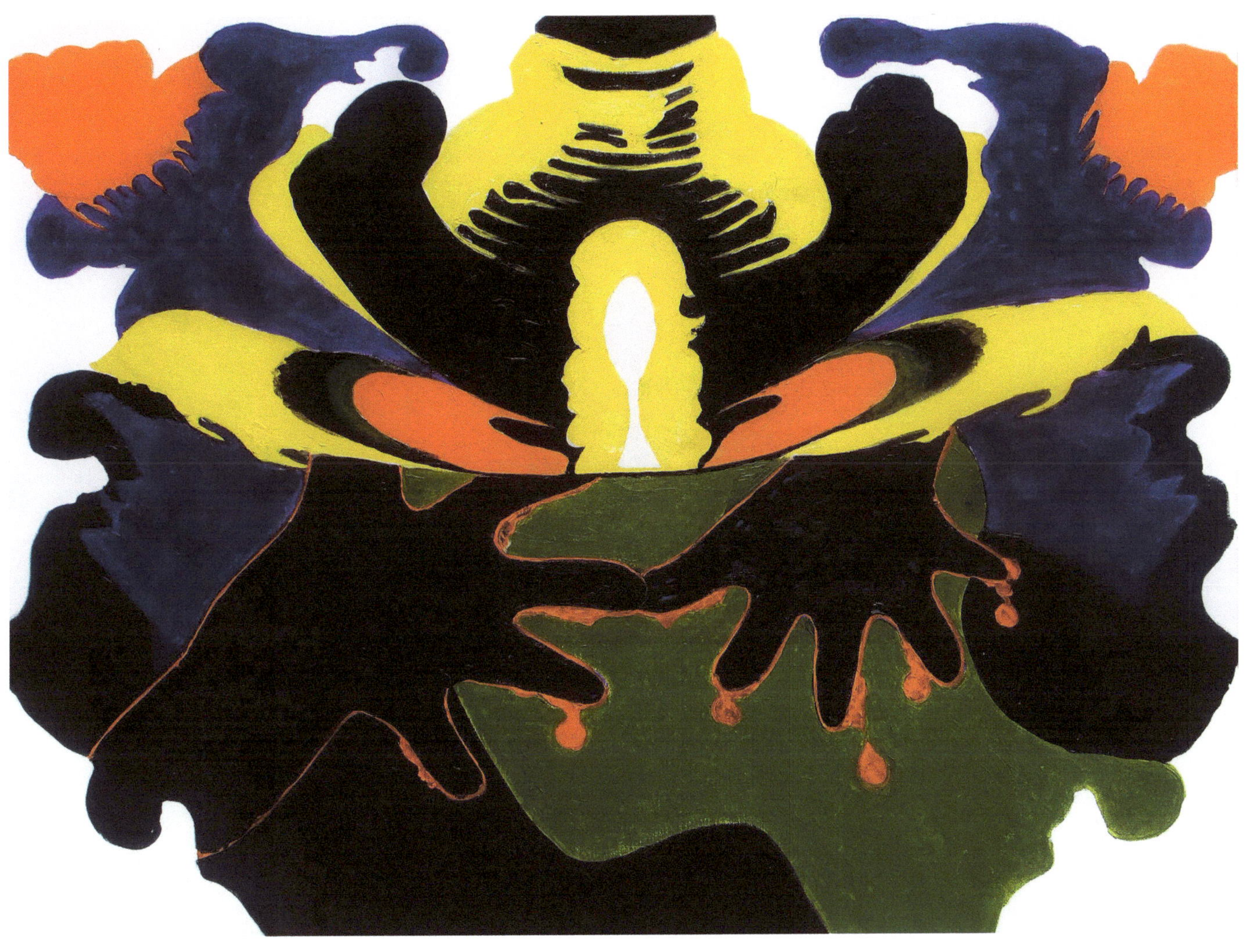

3 Years Old, Hand Fingers

My babyhood was not bright because of my mother's depression and the war. My mother probably wanted to hide me from other people as she was ashamed of my missing eye. In order to avoid the heavy feelings, I must have focused on the green leaves outside of the windows. These brought me to the beauty of fractal shapes that I developed later in life. As you can see my mother's hands and fingers are hiding my face.

Acrylic on Canvas 40x30 inch

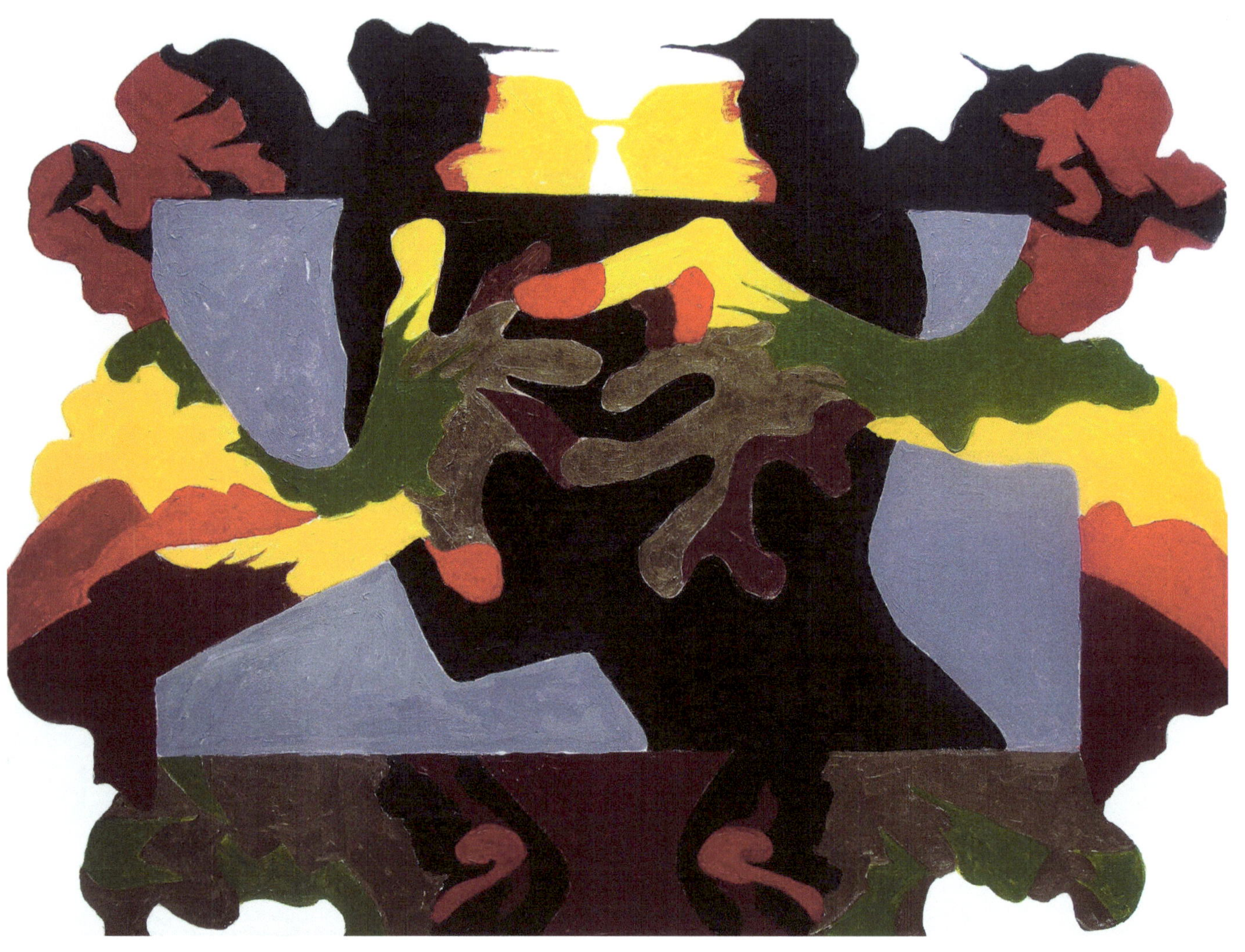

4 Years Old, My Mother's Hands

I was a very contented baby. I took after my father's personality, sometimes identifying with my father freed my feelings. The war is over and it was a relief to be with my father. My father was always proud of his children. He was very sad about my future being in a country and time that stigmatized handicapped children. He never showed these feelings to anyone. We did not have any other family member with a handicap like me. My mother could not nourish herself because of the war yet she felt guilty. As a child, I still grew up well despite my mother's anguished hands.

Acrylic on Canvas 48x36 inch

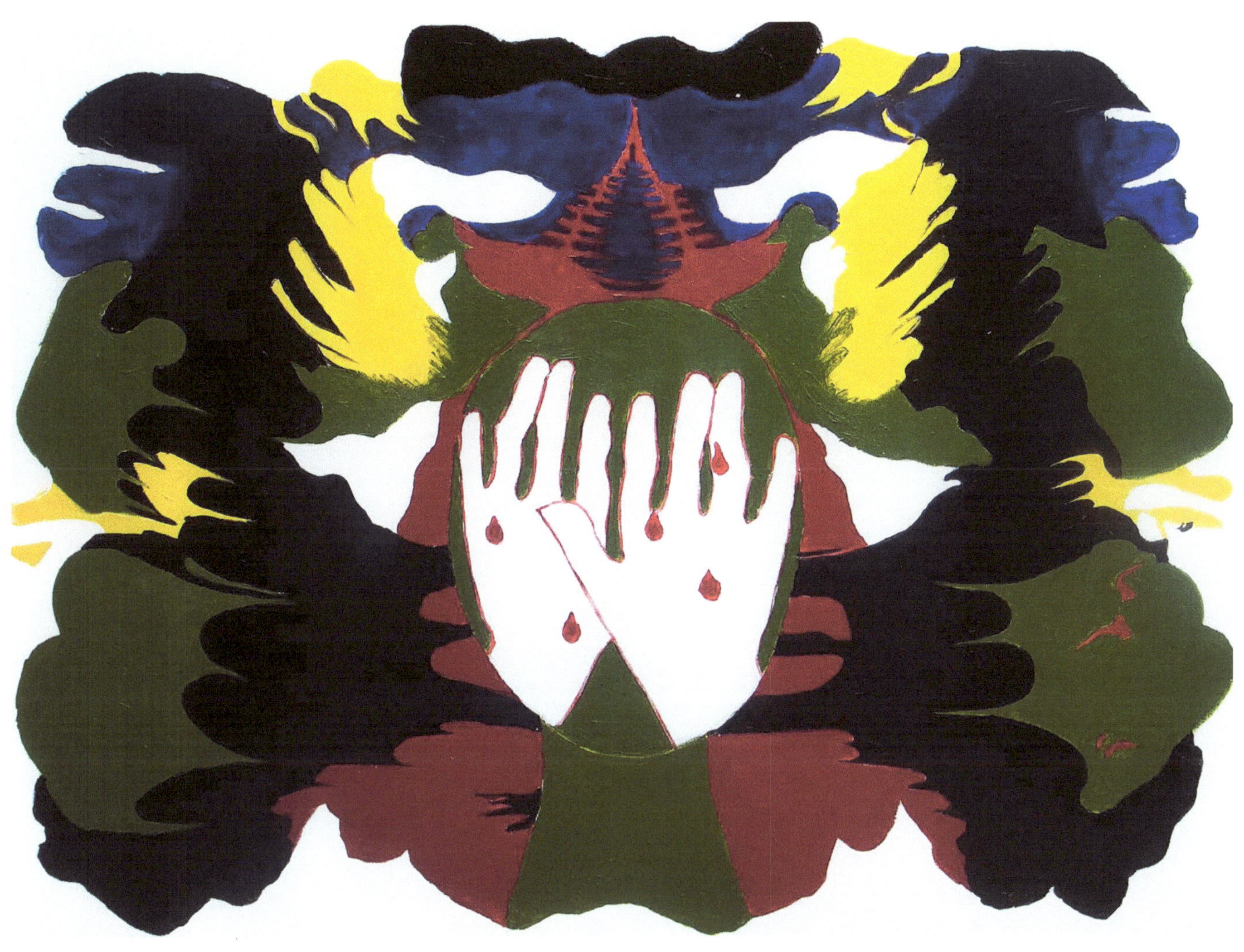

5 Years Old, Growing Up

As I grew up I began to understand the situation related to my handicap better. Sometimes I would put my hands over my face to hide my appearance. I just wanted to be treated the same as any other normal kid. I did not like to be reminded of my handicap nor receive special treatment. My hands are hiding my eyes. I would have to wait until I was 11 years old to improve my looks by having eye surgery.

Acrylic on Canvas 48x36 inch

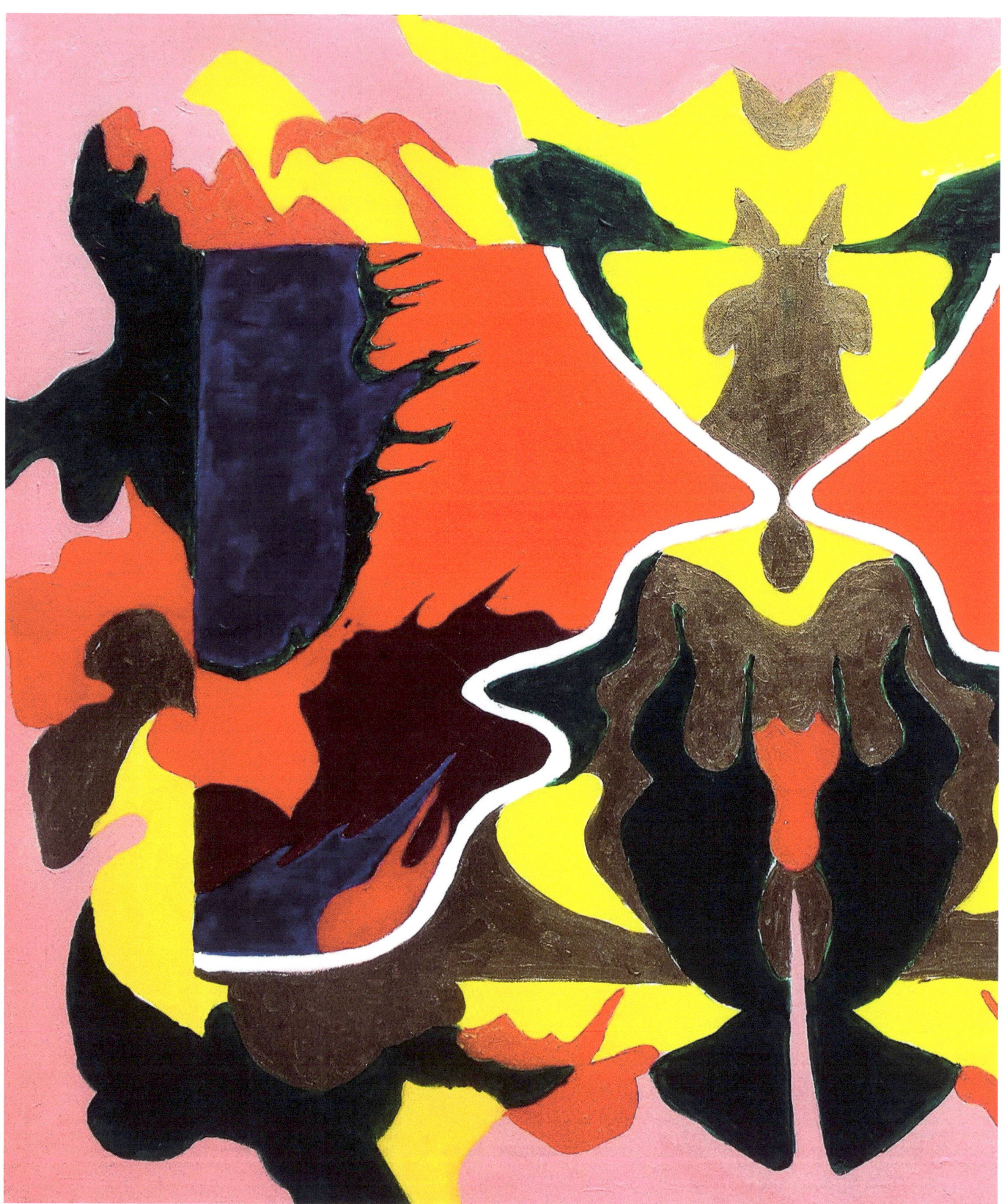

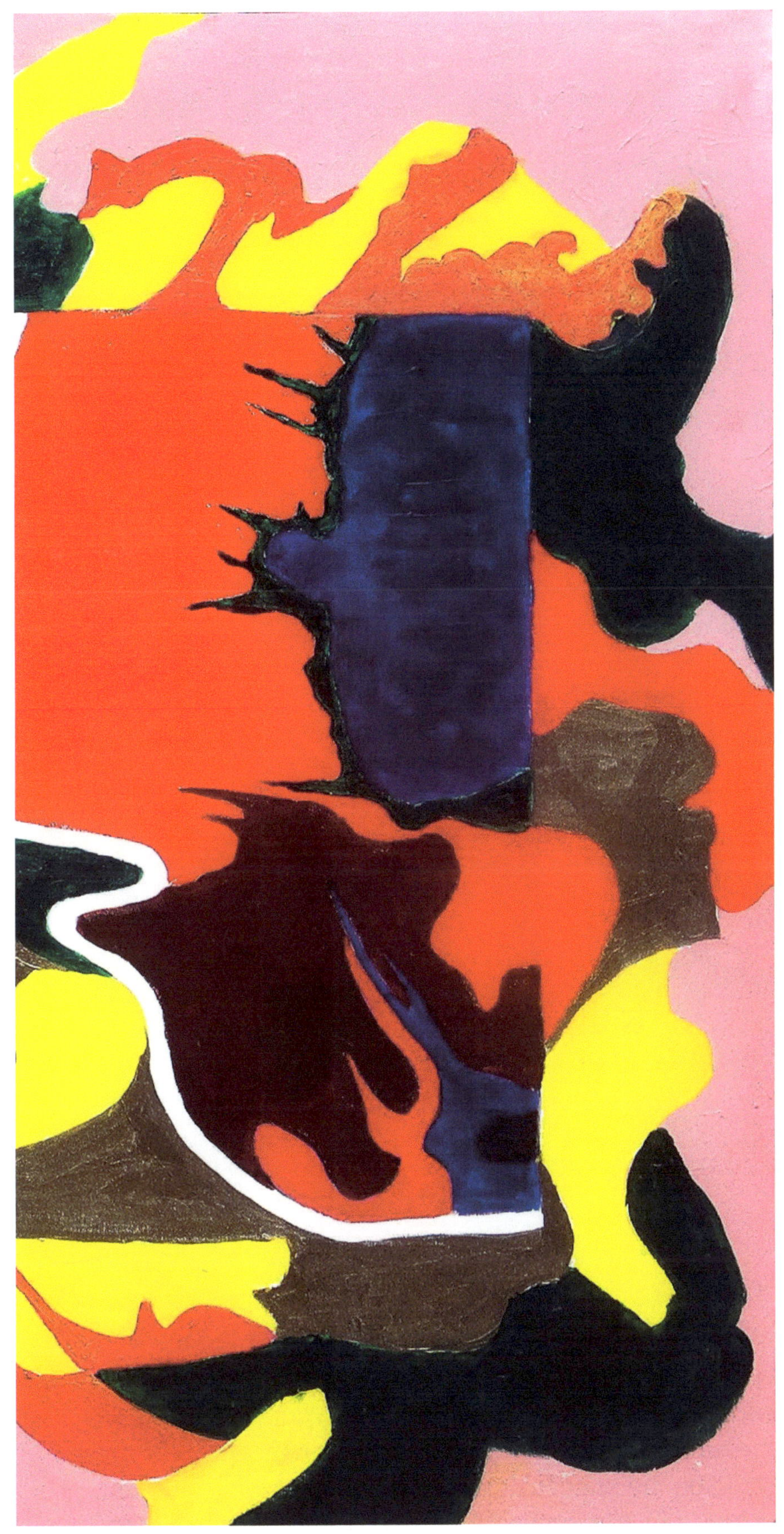

6 Years Old, Shopping

My mother and I went shopping for special clothes for a holiday. I was really excited to get something with a pretty and fashionable design. I think I was a born designer I had very strong preferences. My mother would always buy plain clothes three years older than my actual size in order to keep them for a long time. We walked around the market a couple of times and we had a big disagreement. I was unhappy to see my mother's choice. My mother was angry too and told me it is this one or nothing. So this year I did not get any special clothes.

Acrylic on Canvas 48x36 inch

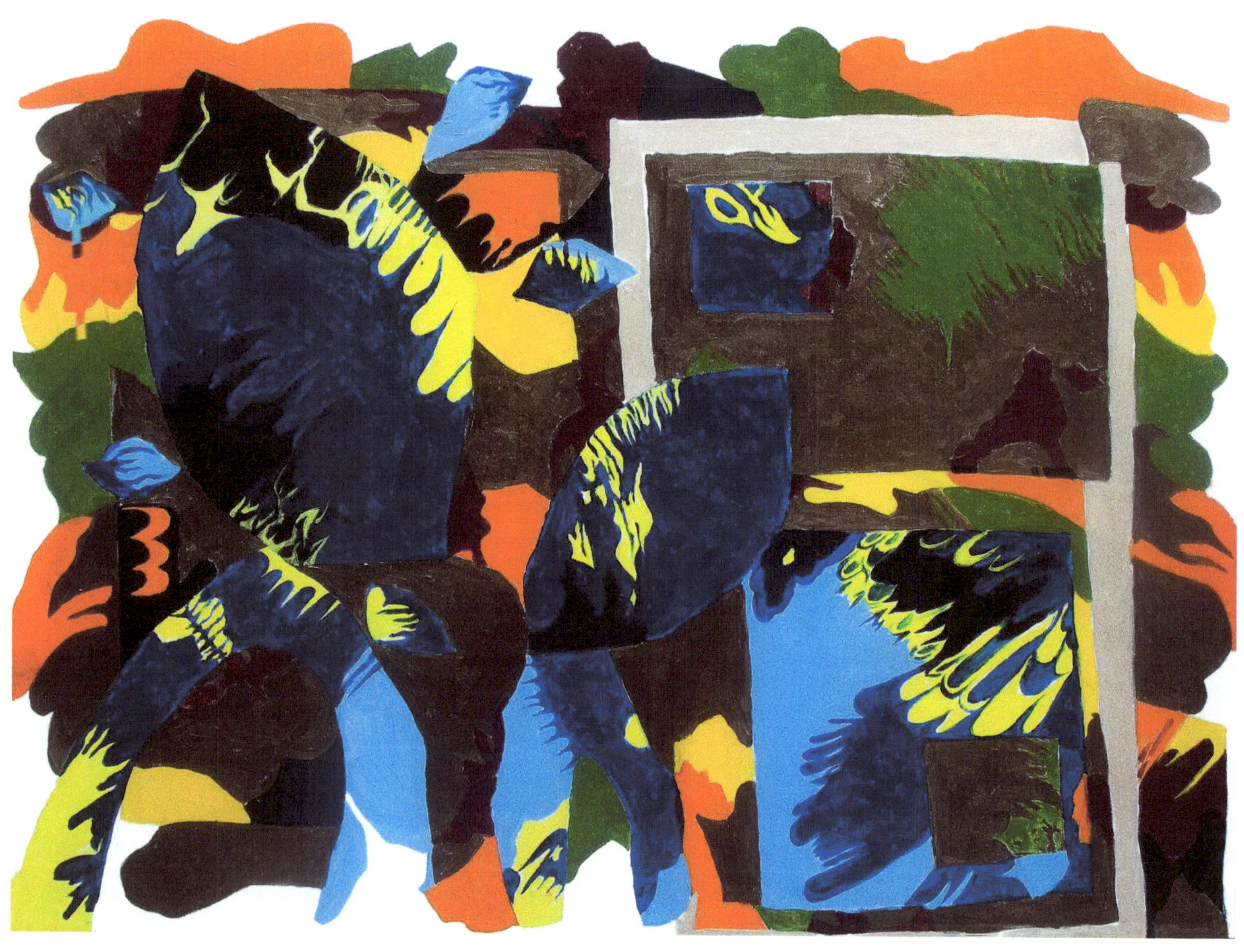

7 Years Old, First Day of School

I grew up with my three sisters and a brother. My sisters and brother always protected me from any hostility related to my handicap. Even now I enjoy small groups of people, no more than 4 or 5. I think that comes from that experience. I have an older sister and two younger sisters. My older sister is six years older than me. She always praised one of my younger sisters. She always thought that my younger sister would be the successful one. Because of this comment, I became the strongest sister by resisting her idea and worked hard to prove myself. Going to school was my opportunity to develop and prove myself. My mother and I walked through the school door. I was excited but I felt my mother's gloom hanging over me.

Acrylic on Canvas 48x36 inch

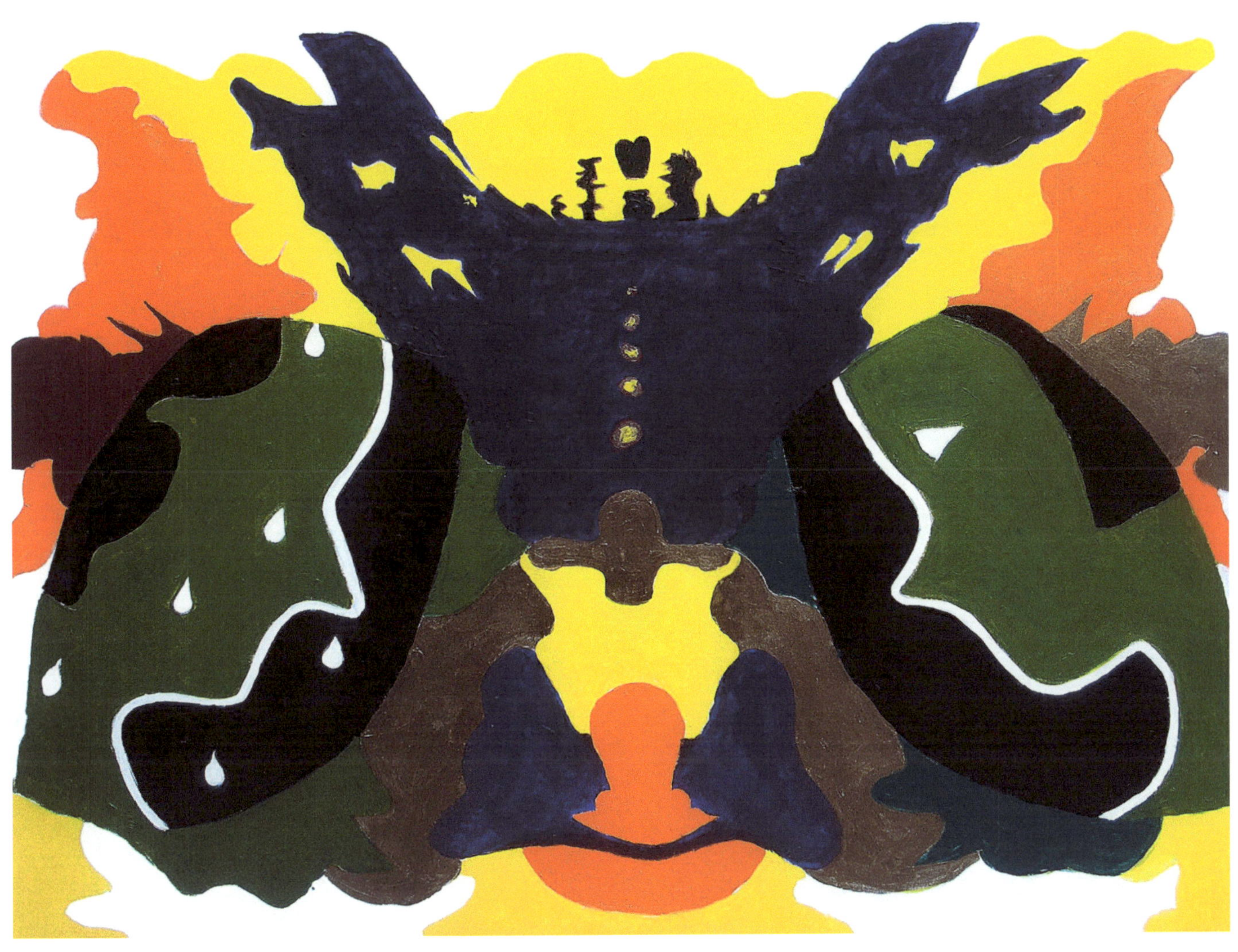

7 Years Old, My Mother's Sweat

My mother and I were walking to the school hand in hand. I could feel my mother's feelings clouding over thinking of me and my damaged eye. My mother and father said that since I had to be independent I had to study and they would support me to the end of my study. I was more prepared than my mother and I was thinking I can do much better than my mother. At the last step into the door, my mother was sweating hard and had a hard time stepping over into the public space.

Acrylic on Canvas 48x36 inch

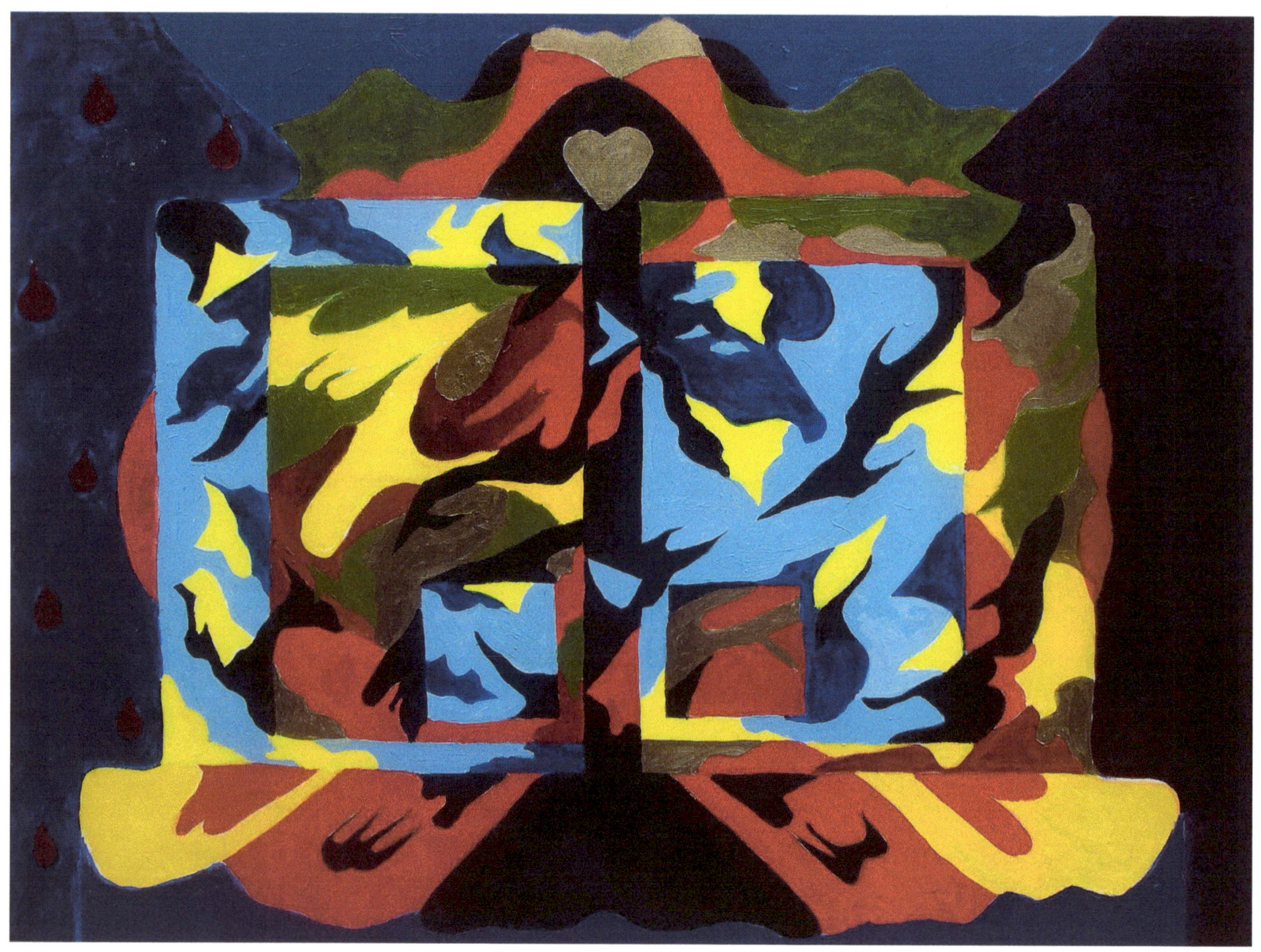

8 Years Old, Woman Doctor

My parents always thought I should have a good profession in case I cannot get married because of my eye. They thought that I should be a woman doctor. The woman doctor idea sounded very scary to me but I liked my parent's thoughts. The double doors enter into the school as a place for me to flourish. I became a very good student and planned to get into the best school.

Acrylic on Canvas 48x36 inch

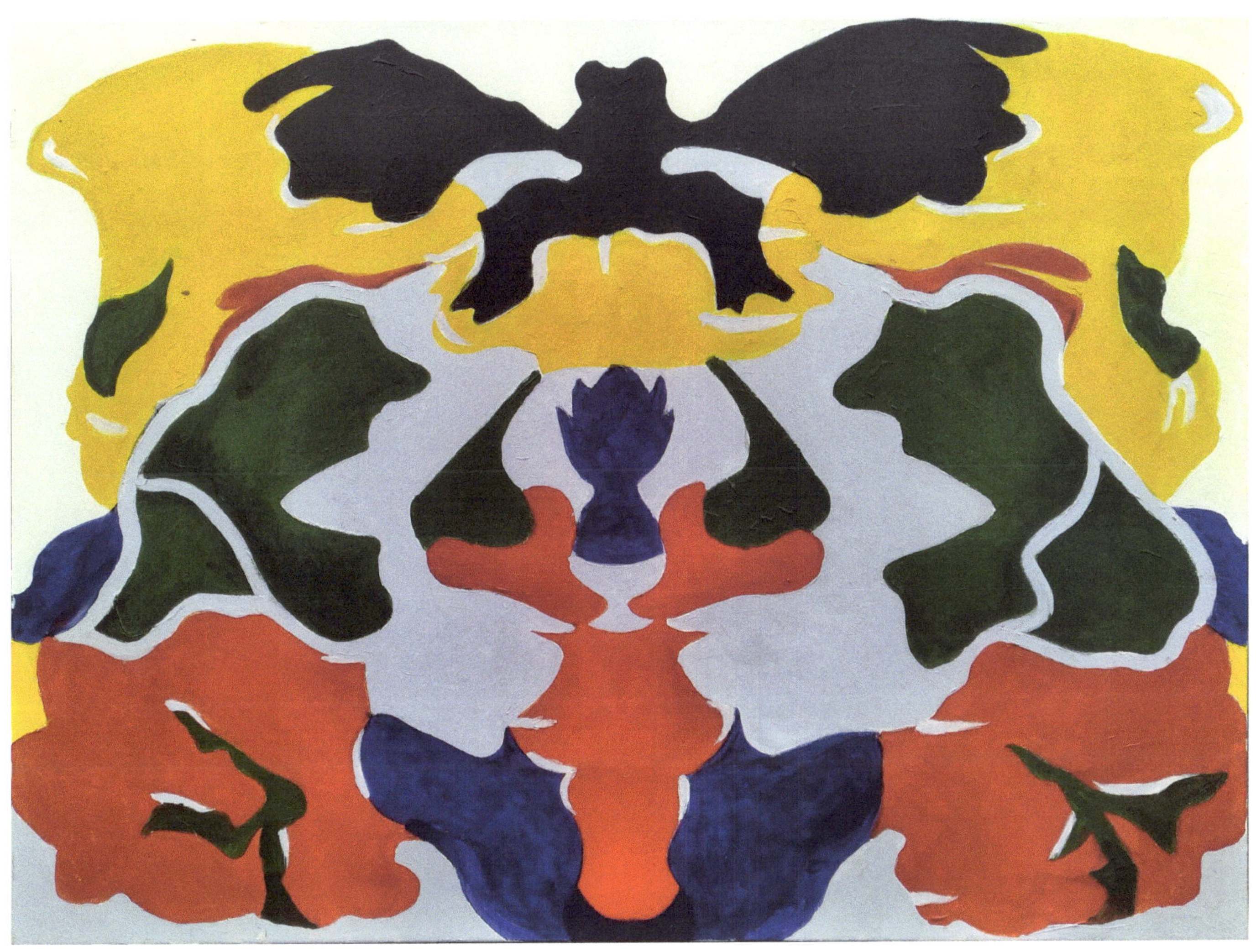

9 Years Old, Frustration

It seems the time is going to go really slow as I wait for surgery to improve my disfigured eye. One day a women scolded me for having such a handicapped look. She said "go to your mother and do something about it". I did not say to her that the surgery had to wait until I was 11 years old. I was frustrated and not sure what the surgery was and what would be done. I could not imagine myself after the surgery.

Acrylic on Canvas 48x36 inch

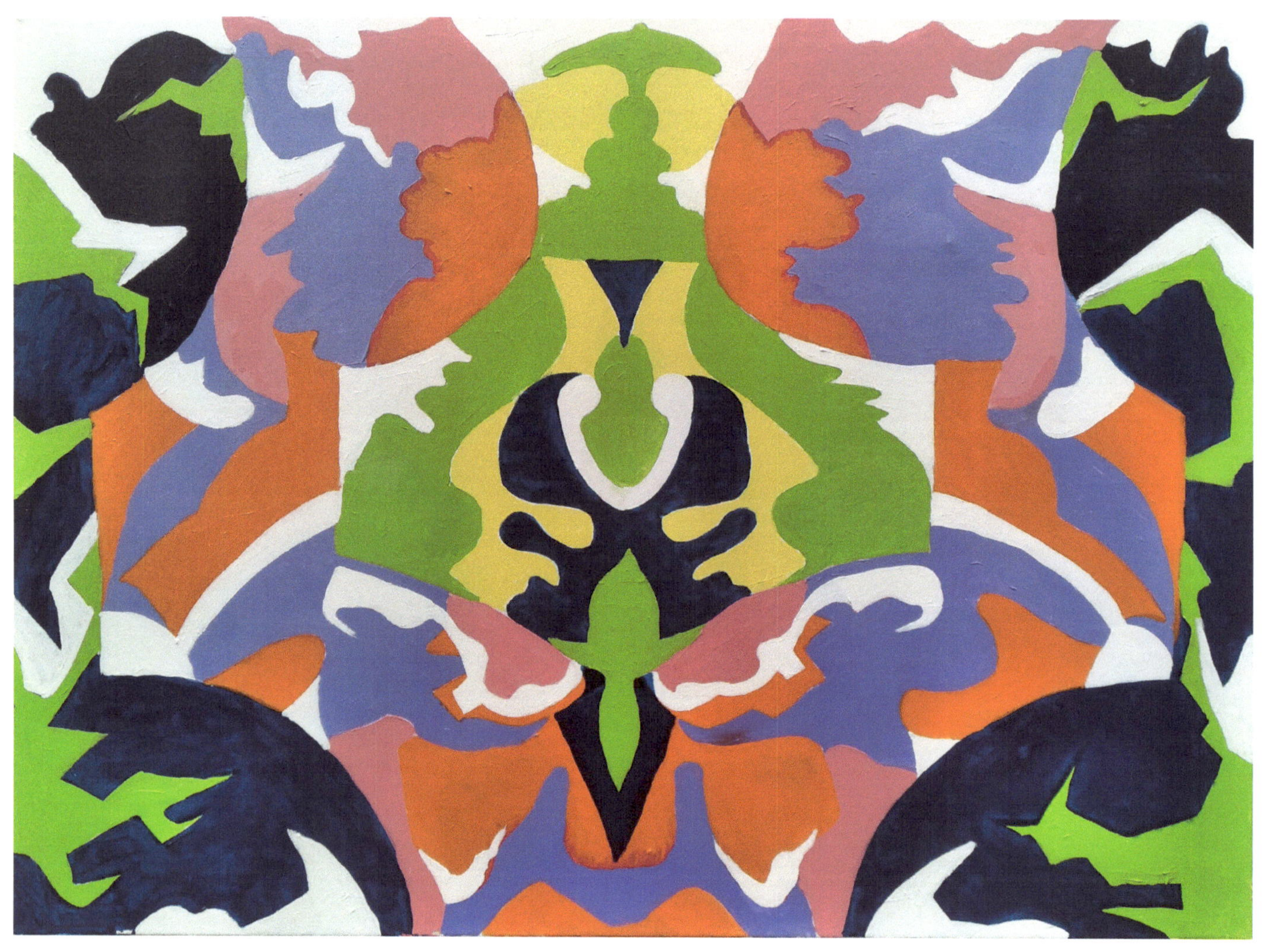

10 Years Old, The Boyfriend?

I had met a boy who was so kind to me. We hang around together and walk home together. He always protects me and my friends. When the bad boys steal our playthings he will go and get things back from the bad boys. I wondered how I got so much attention from the boy and I was not a victim of discrimination anymore. I was grateful to have good friends. This painting shows the exciting blossoming feelings of friendship surrounded by secure protection.

Acrylic on Canvas 48x36 inch

Chapter 2 – Surgery and growing up

At 11 years old I had surgery to remove the undeveloped eye and correct the eyelid and surrounding areas. I was also fitted with an artificial eye that although not perfect did help to make me more normal. To me this was a major change. I looked pretty, I was a young girl, I could do young girl things. My life changed.

I developed more outward confidence. I already had a strong personality that helped me in my early years. Now I began to have real confidence and security in my interaction with other people I felt I could interact as equals and not have to be super strong and defend myself. Friendships began to develop. My life opened up.

As I developed into adolescence and young adulthood I became more confident. I was a beautiful young woman. I was proud of my developing body and I thrived at university surrounded by intelligent people who accepted me completely, without special sympathy or kindness but as an equal.

The paintings in this chapter cover years 11 to 22, school, university and my first job.

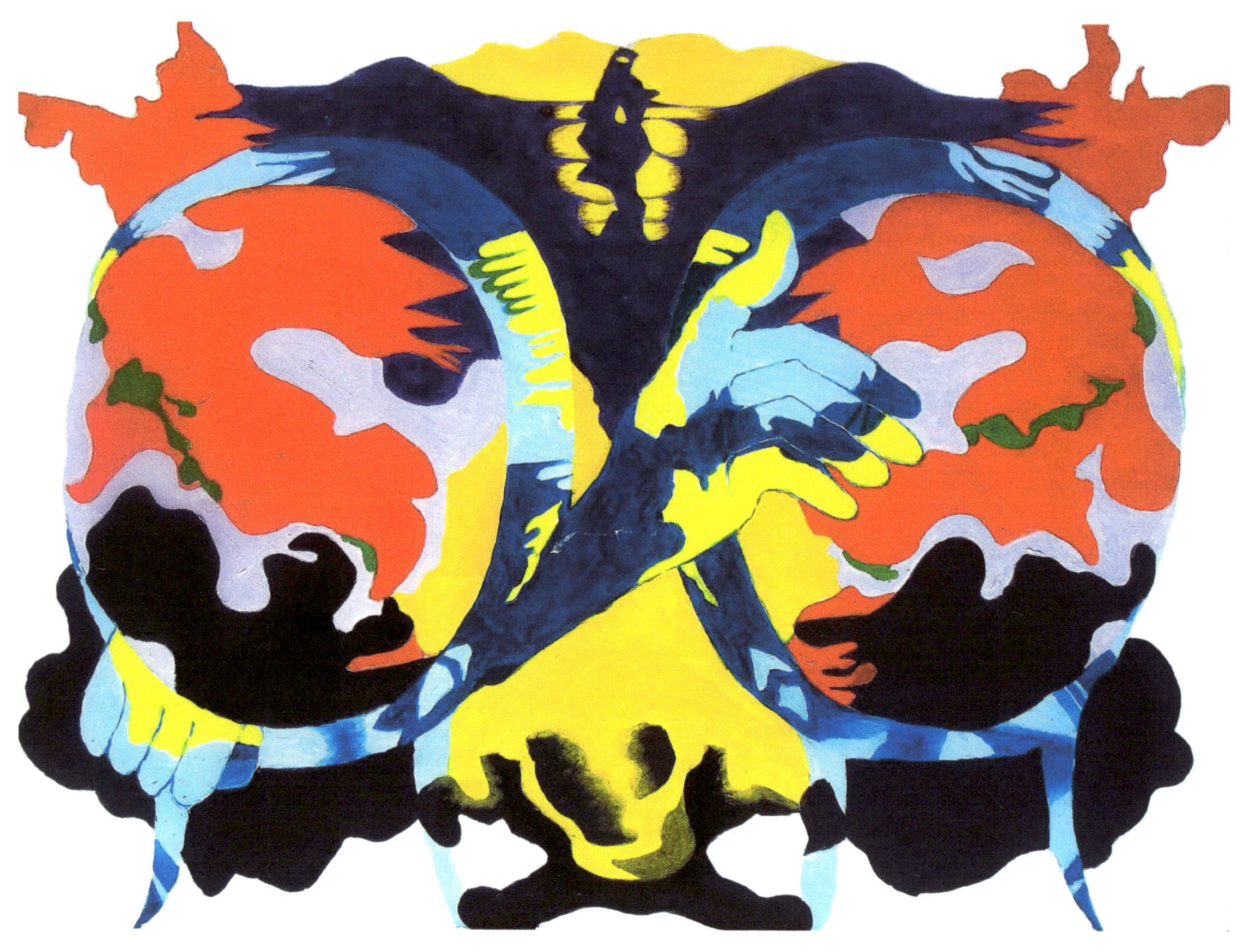

11 Years Old, Eye Operation

The eye operation changed a lot of things for me. I no longer had only one eye. It was not obvious that I had a prosthetic eye. I looked like a normal girl at first glance. The operation was very hard but well worth it as it improved my confidence enormously. One hand connects the eyes to my life story. Everything is now bright and challenging.

Acrylic on Canvas 48x36 inch

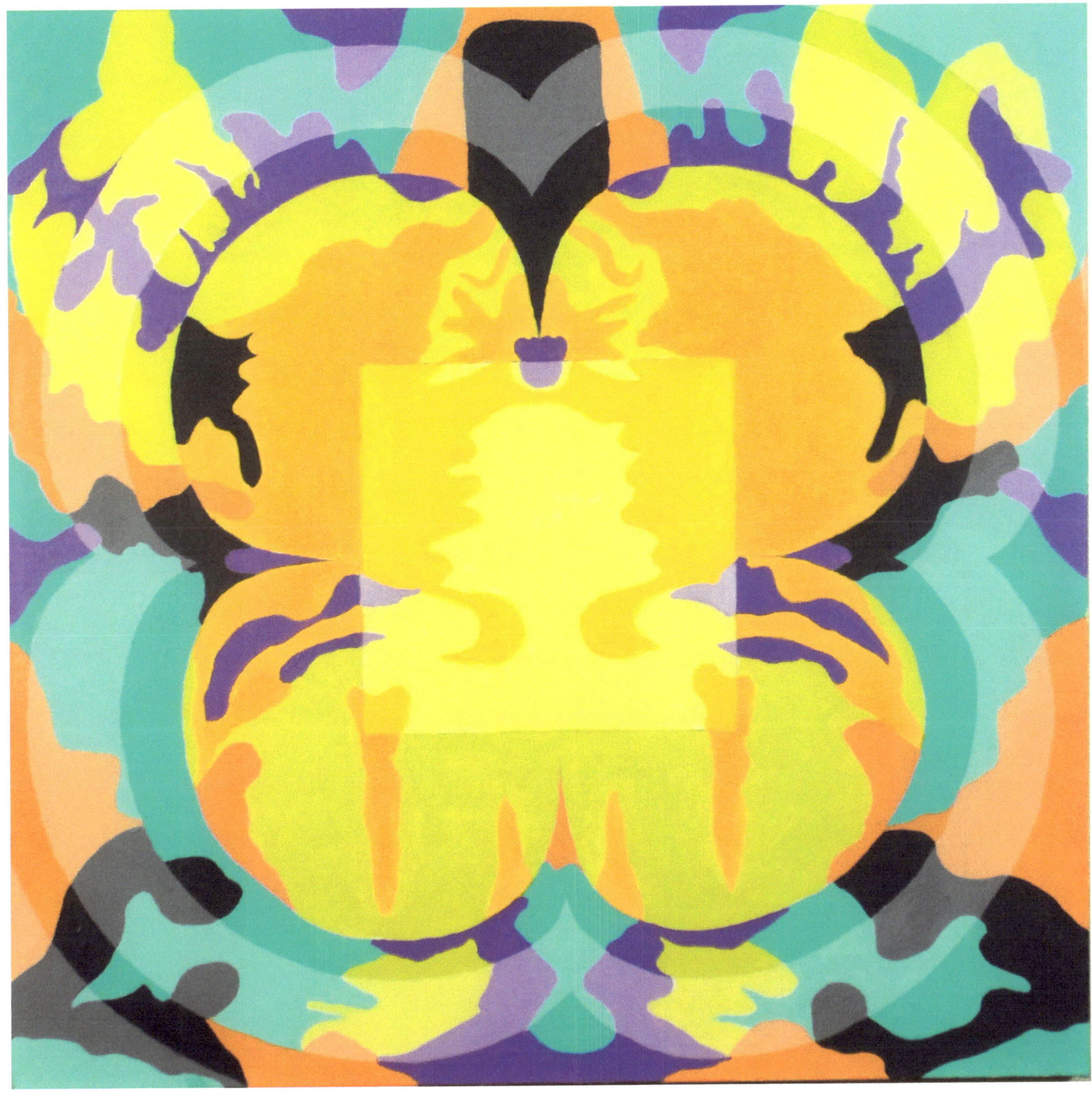

12 Years Old, Rebirth

It is a rebirth to me! I did not realize that everything would change for me after my eye surgery. I am a normal girl! A normal girl waiting for good things to happen to me. My future seemed rosy. These symbolic eggs are dividing into four parts. I am excited about this new change. How wonderful and beautiful I feel. A new beginning.

Acrylic on Canvas 48x48 inch

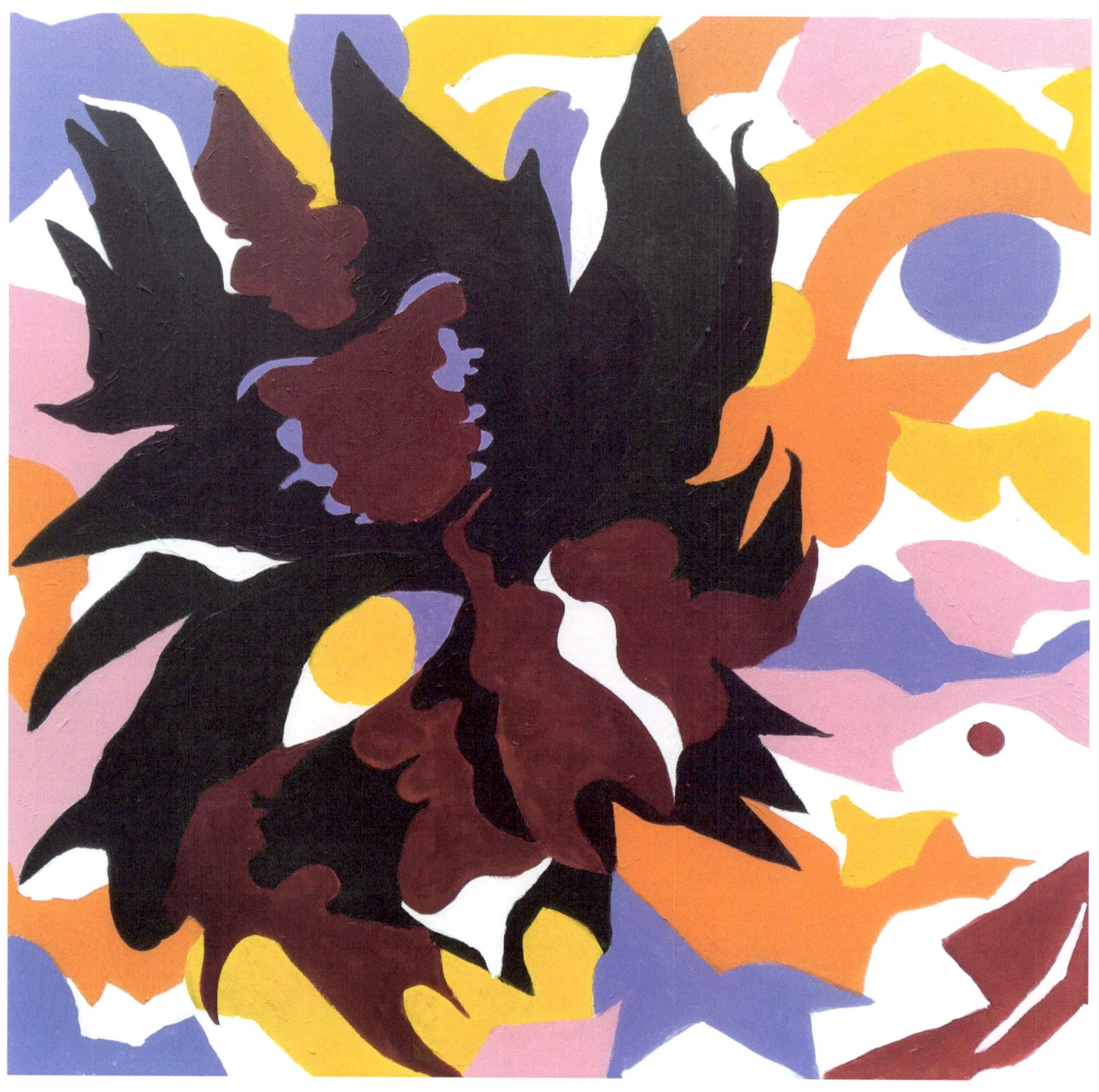

13 Years Old, The Confidence

I have had surgery for my prosthetic right eye for some time now. I had to wait until I was 11 years old for the surgery since my bones were developing. My face now looks so much better and my handicap is not noticed at all. I began to have confidence in my appearance. I began to look prettier and prettier. I am having pink dreamy thoughts just like other girls at this age. I am expanding physically and psychologically with exciting colors and shapes in the painting.

Acrylic on Canvas 36x36 inch

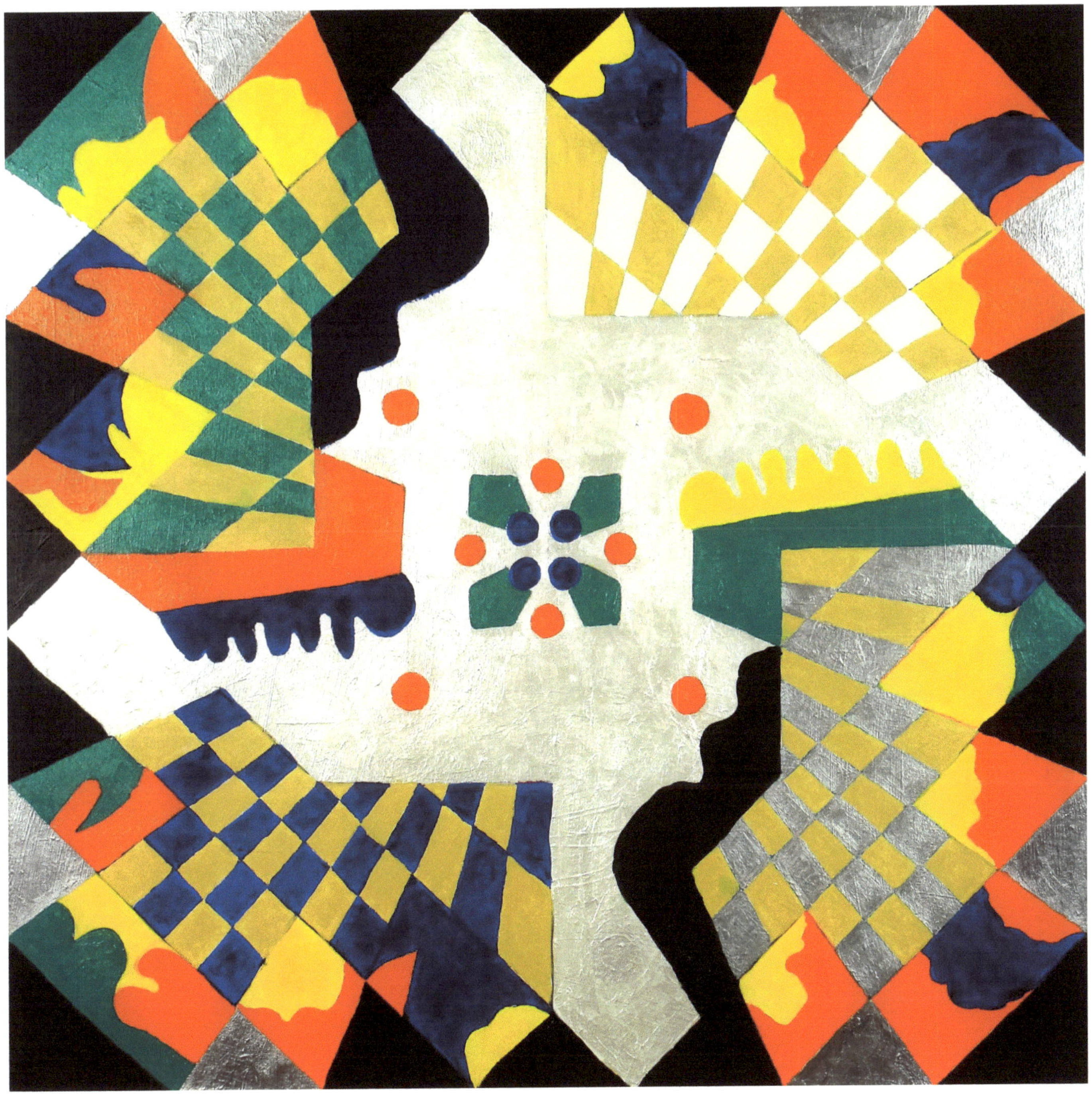

14 Years Old, Beautiful Life

I am beginning to think about my future with rosy color. I want to be a good friend to my career, and try to organize my life. I want to be strong and step down firmly to the ground with my two feet firmly on the ground and grow up. The organization is moving around and circling around. The beautiful colors are always around me. The background is jolly and exciting.

Acrylic on Canvas 48x48 inch

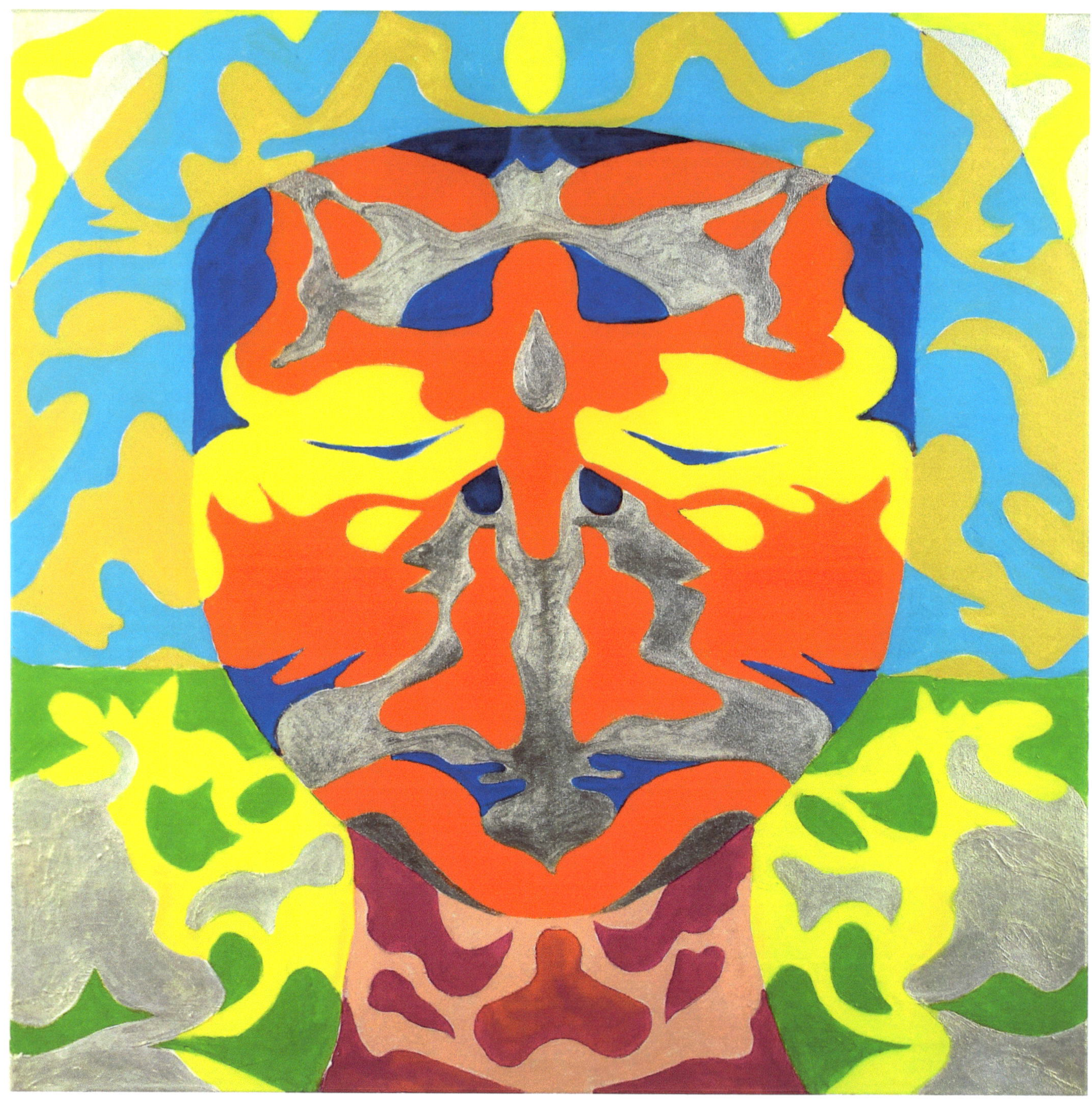

15 Years Old, Dreamy Girl

Every teenager goes through the period of many beautiful dreams about the future. I was a realistic dreamer so I want to translate the dream into a realistic one. We used to talk together as friends and compare our dreams. I had many dreams, like in this painting, I was in a happy and serene mood when I dream about the future.

Acrylic on Canvas 36x36 inch

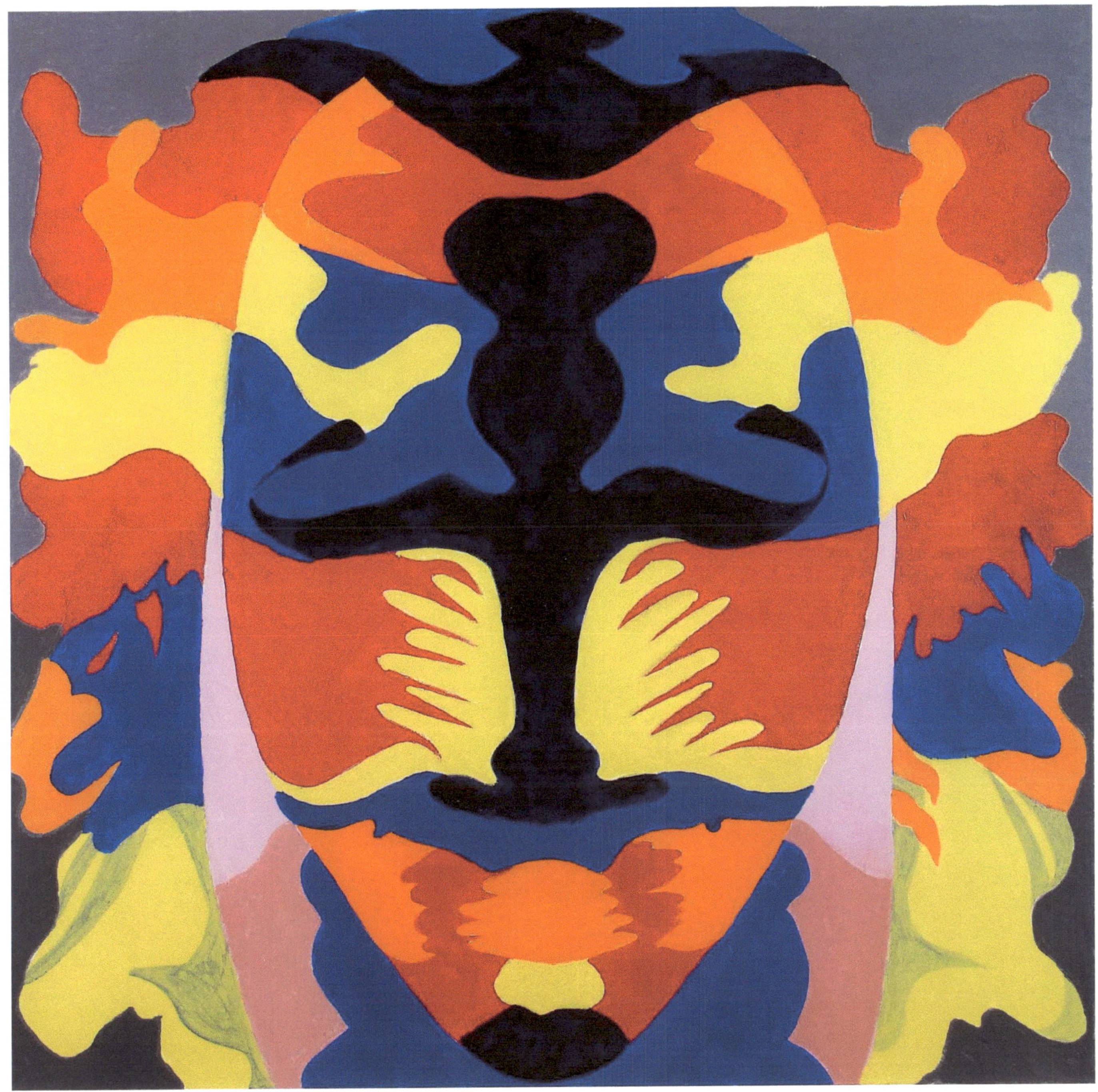

16 Years Old, Beautiful Woman

I became a beautiful woman! Now I plan to be a successful human being. I know that I can succeed in whatever I can try and be a person. I can be a beautiful pianist and artist if I want to be. I do not know yet what I want to be but I know I will succeed to be if I want. I think that I am beautiful enough to engage in the world. All the colors and shapes of the world are mine to work with. Now it depends on what I want to be.

Acrylic on Canvas 36x36 inch

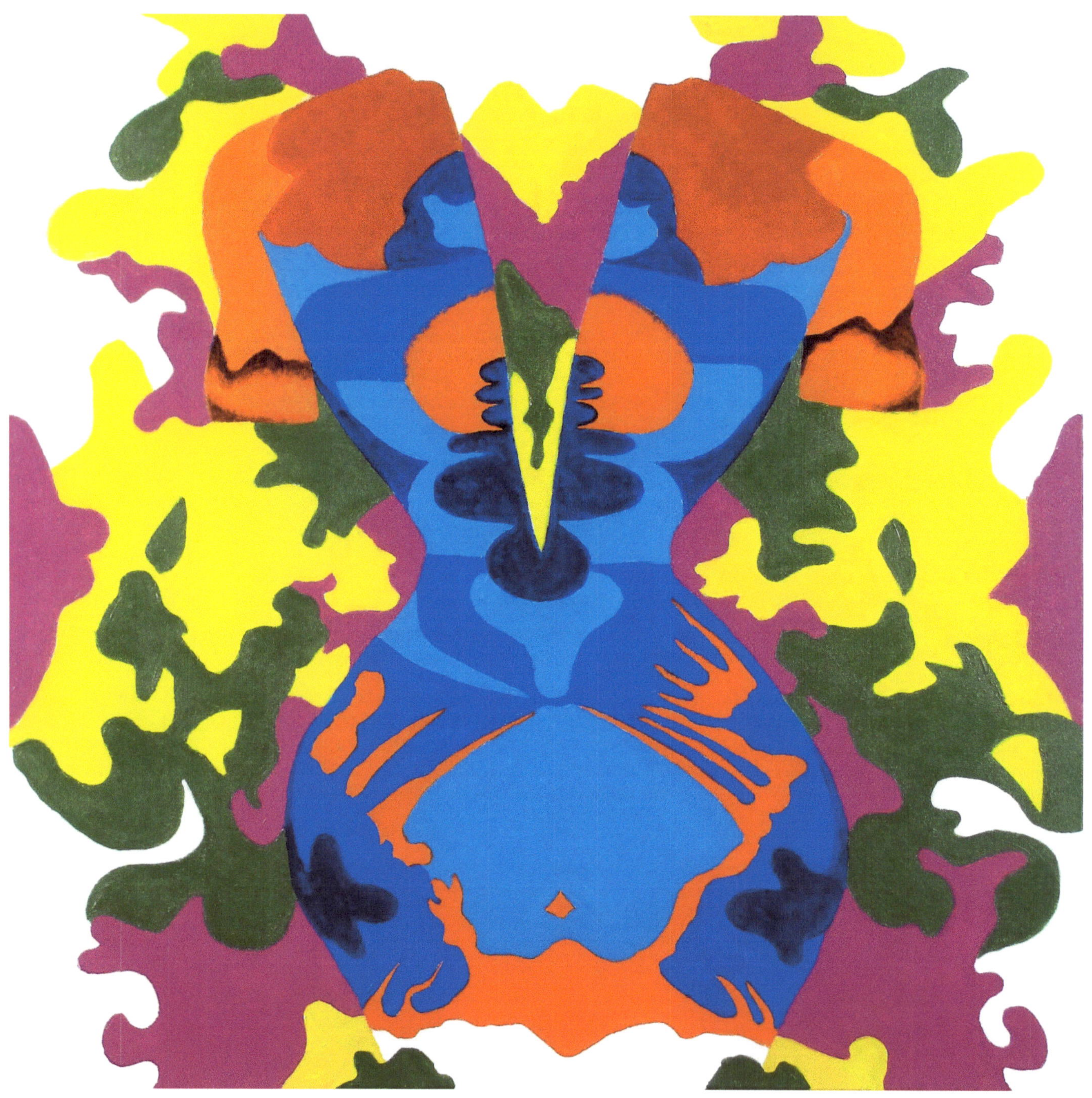

17 Years Old, The Body

I look at my body in the mirror. I have an exceptionally balanced figure. To my surprise, I was proud of it. Like a butterfly, I can stretch my big wings and body. My curvy body looks sporty too. I can dream about the design of the clothes and their colors.

Acrylic on Canvas 36x36 inch

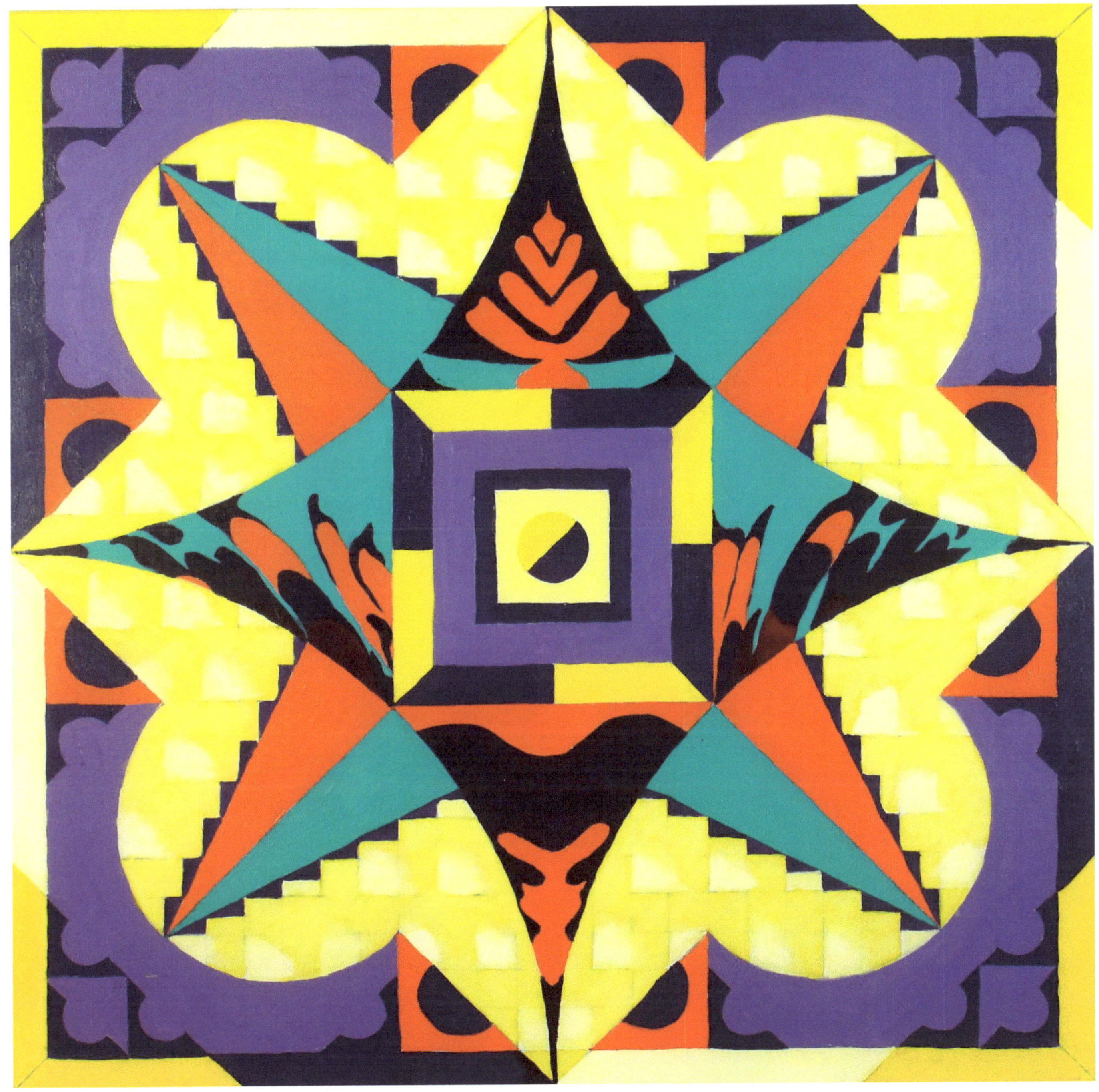

18 Years Old, University Girl

First year in university! I pass the entry exam and I am in the best university. I study German literature and language. I want to go to the mountains and play guitar. I worked very hard to get into the University. I decided to learn more about life and adventure. Traveling with three or four friends is the best way. Life is tessellated together. Meeting boys and traveling together is really fun. Although I have not met a boy who is following me.

Acrylic on Canvas 36x36 inch

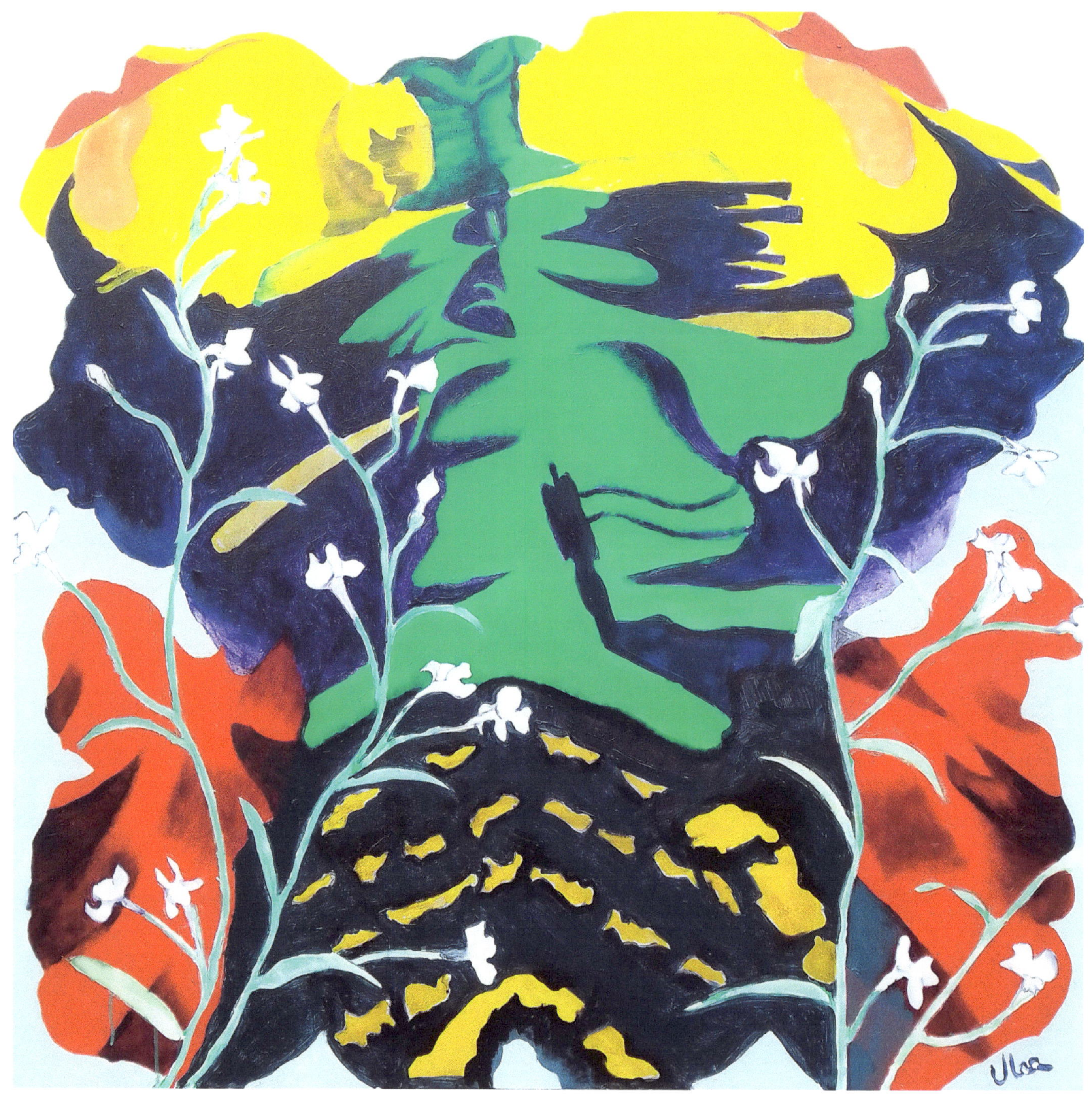

19 Years Old, Mountain Girl

I was called as a mountain girl. I spent a lot of my time traveling and climbing the mountains. We were a group of 4 or 5 people and spent the weekends traveling together. We are giggling and spending the time laughing together. Like this….. we are experiencing life on our own terms. All these scenes are imprinted in my mind. Wondering how nature can be so beautiful and harmonious while at the same time it looks haphazard.

Acrylic on Canvas 48x48 inch

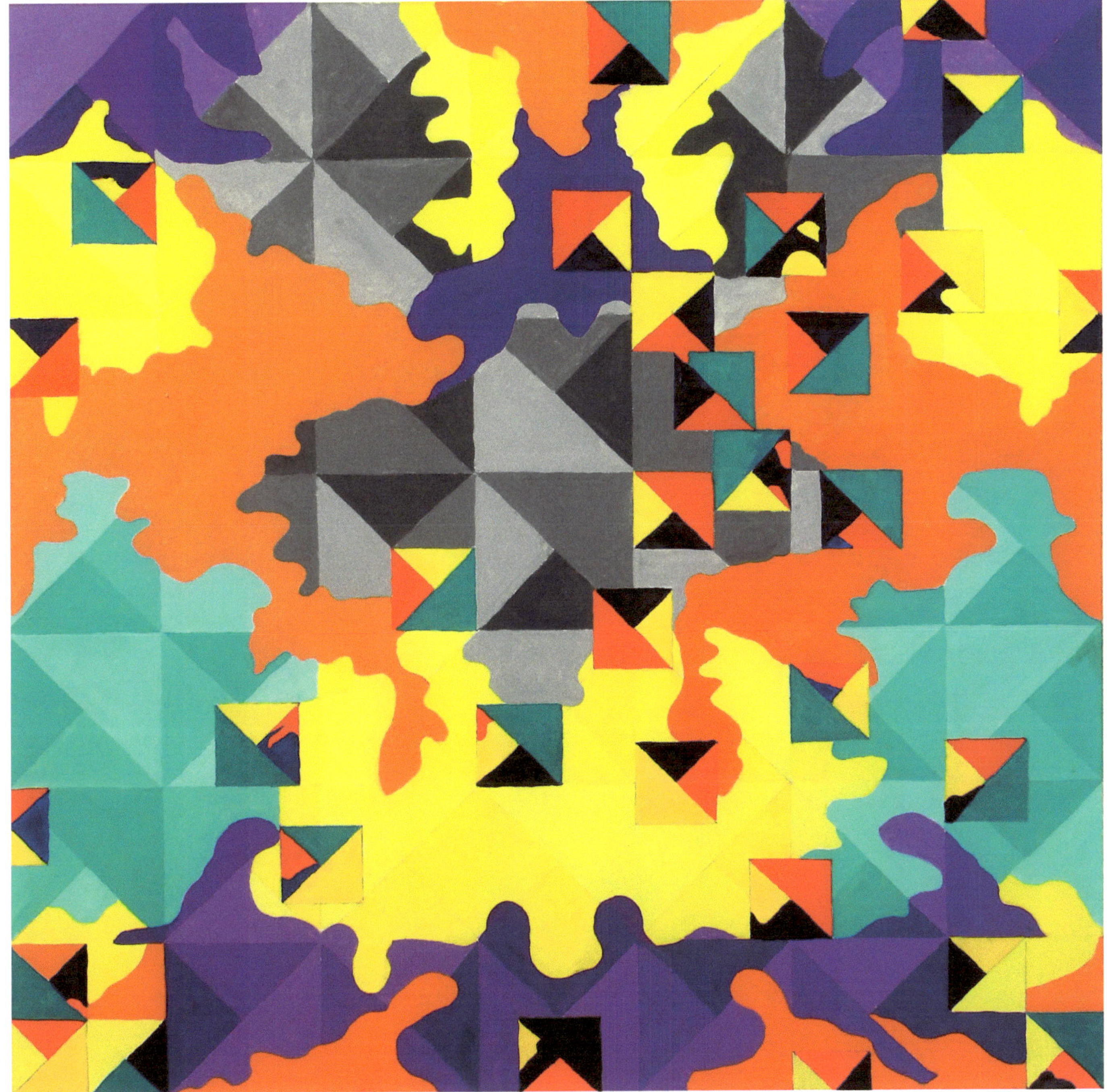

20 Years Old, 3rd Year at College

I am beginning to realize that life is complicated. I really do not know everything in life at all. But I see things in a positive way even if sometimes I hover between positive and negative feelings. Mostly I am the happy and lucky one. You can see the happiness and complicated interaction from the general tone of this painting.

Acrylic on Canvas 48x48 inch

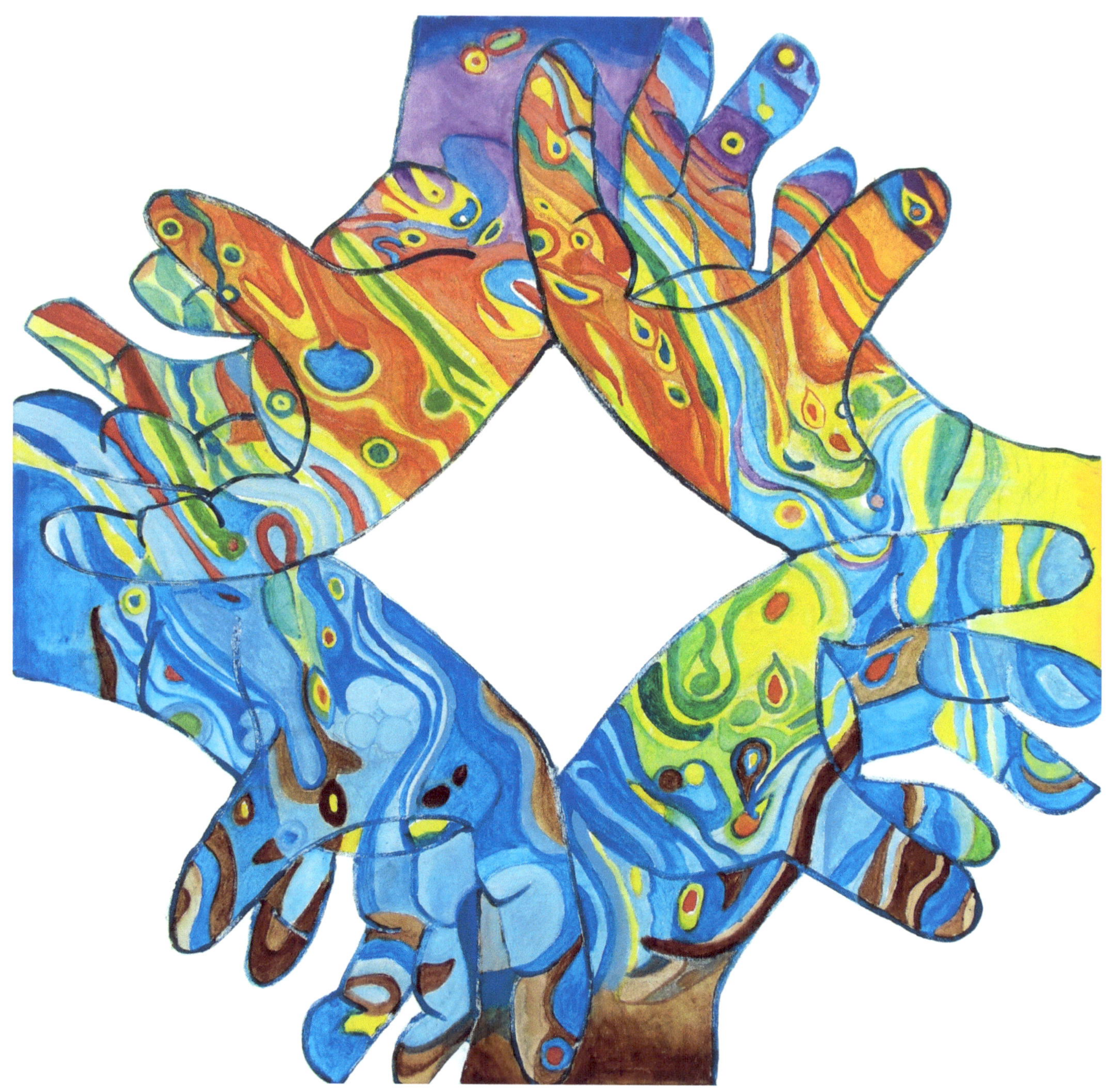

21 Years Old, Senior Year at College

We are all senior year! We are all surprised at the time-lapse in University life. All are anxious and waiting for what will be the next chapter in life. All the conversations we had and so many trips to the mountains are in our hearts. I am anxious about how I will be accepted into society. But I was not the only one and we all supported each other.

Acrylic on Canvas 36x36 inch

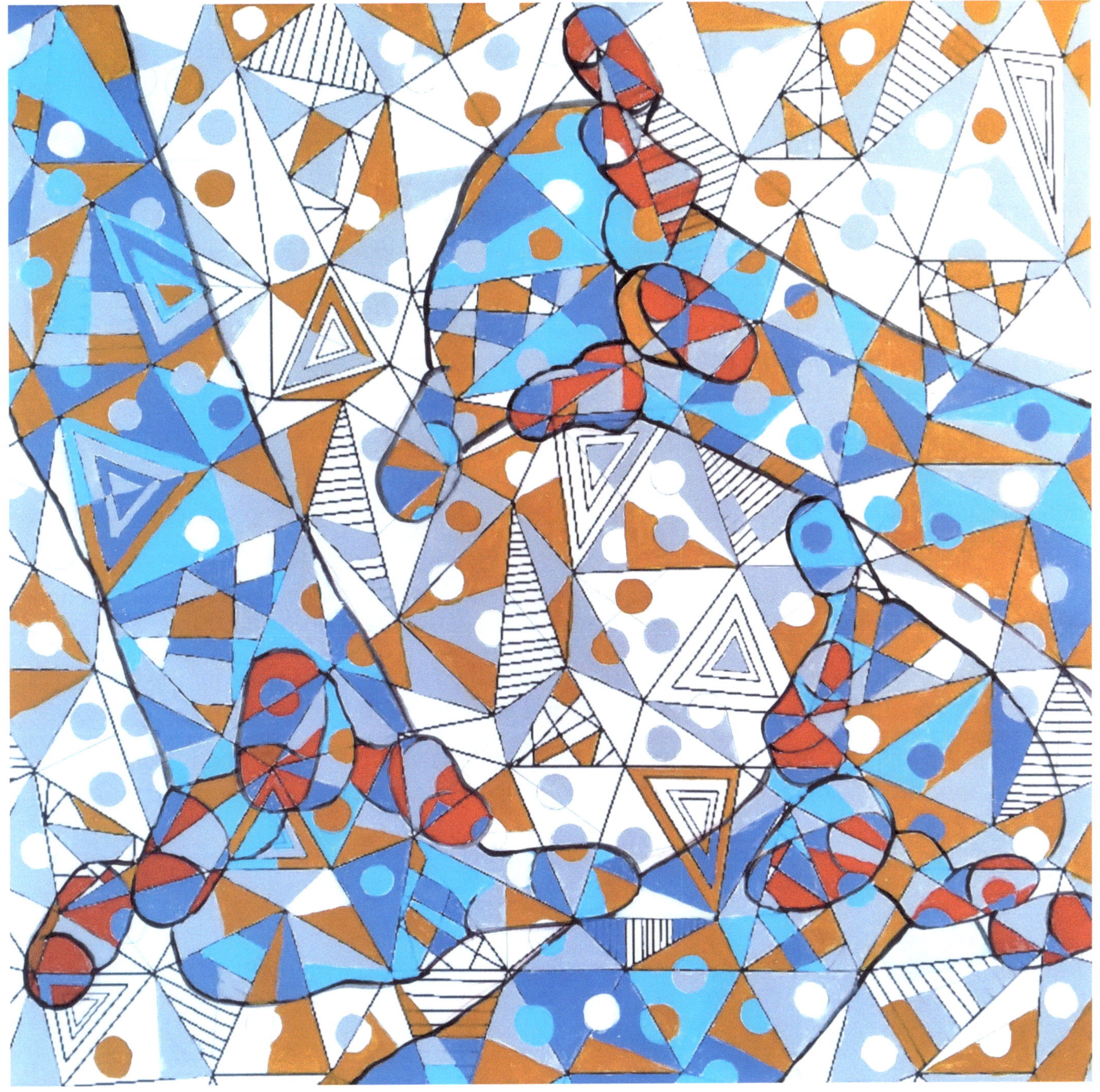

22 Years Old, Working in the Bank

Working in the bank was a great experience. I enjoyed getting the same pay as men while working in an American Bank. Everything had to be exactly balanced every day making a total of zero. I am excited about having a job and having experience as an adult. I wonder if I will be totally accepted in my job and life. In this painting, the pressures of job and life are layered on the background of intricate bank details and life interactions.

Acrylic on Canvas 36x36 inch

Chapter 3 – Married, Study in Paris, Career

I am now an adult and married to a wonderful husband who shared my passion for traveling the world. He was a United States citizen serving as a lawyer for the army in Korea. Our first adventure was moving to Colorado for a short while, then a big move to Paris in France. The art and architecture in Paris had a big influence on me. I set my career in motion by studying Interior Architecture with a French influence.

I took this influence back to the USA when I returned and studied for a BFA in Interior Design at Parson's School of Design. I did not know it at that time but this was the start of my life and career in New York City. The study was hard, I was facing the challenges one by one.

My job as an Interior Designer was at Skidmore Owings and Merrill (SOM), one of the leading architecture companies in New York City. I thrived at the work and gained confidence. I eventually got frustrated at following other peoples design visions and being brave decided to set up my own Company.

I started my own business U Lee Johnson and Associates (ULJA) and worked with like minded designers. I had the freedom to express my own thoughts and designs.

I was living my dream and life was wonderful. I was confident and full of hope for the future. I did not know that serious and disastrous life challenges were to come.

The paintings in this chapter cover years 23 through 34 and illustrate a young adult developing full of confidence.

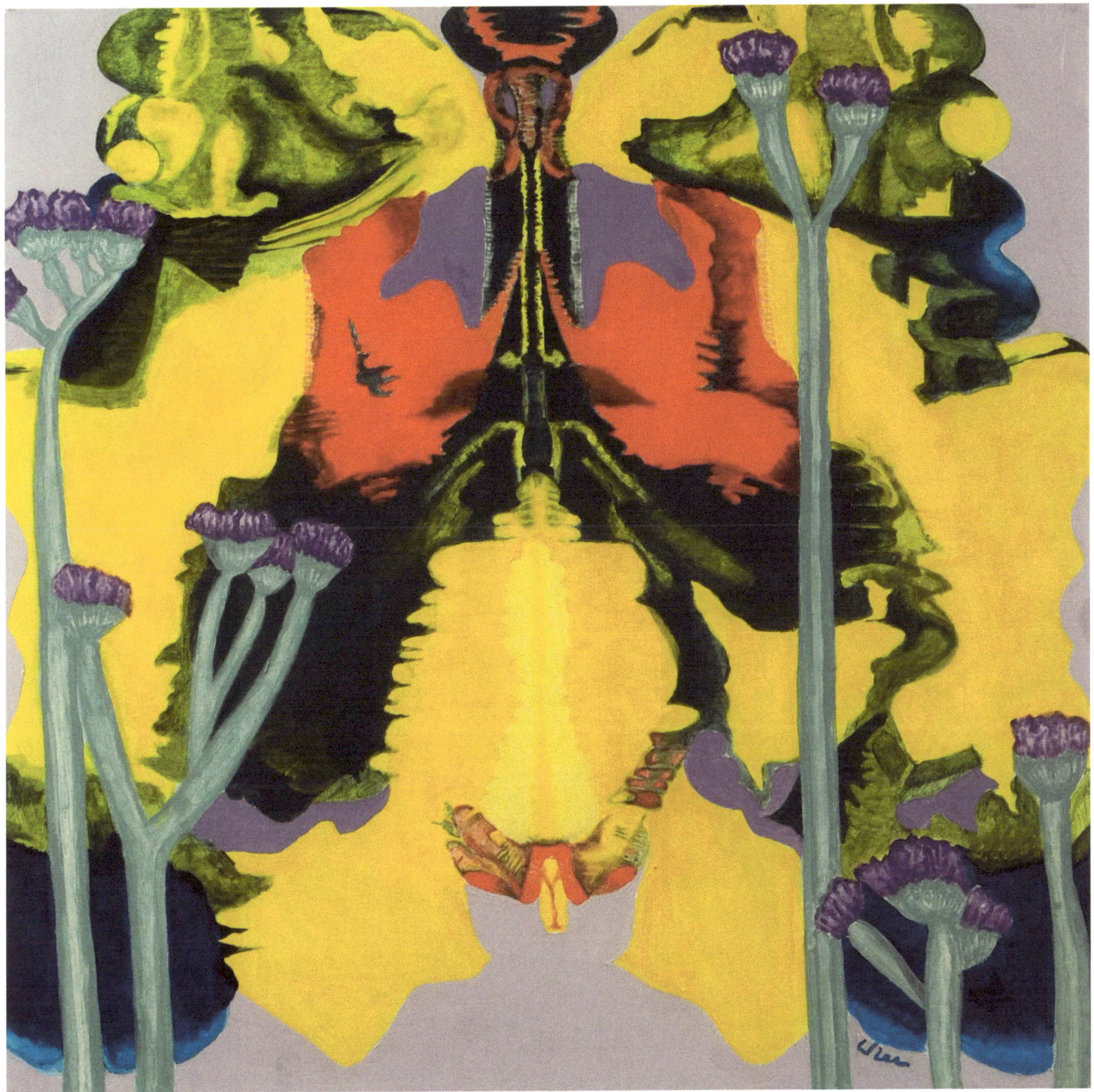

23 Years Old, BoA

As I planned, I worked in society for two years. Even though it was an isolated bank experience I could feel the atmosphere of a working life. The fulfillment comes with a competitive environment. This painting represents the complex organization of the work and products some of which grow into potential flowers.

Acrylic on Canvas 36x36 inch

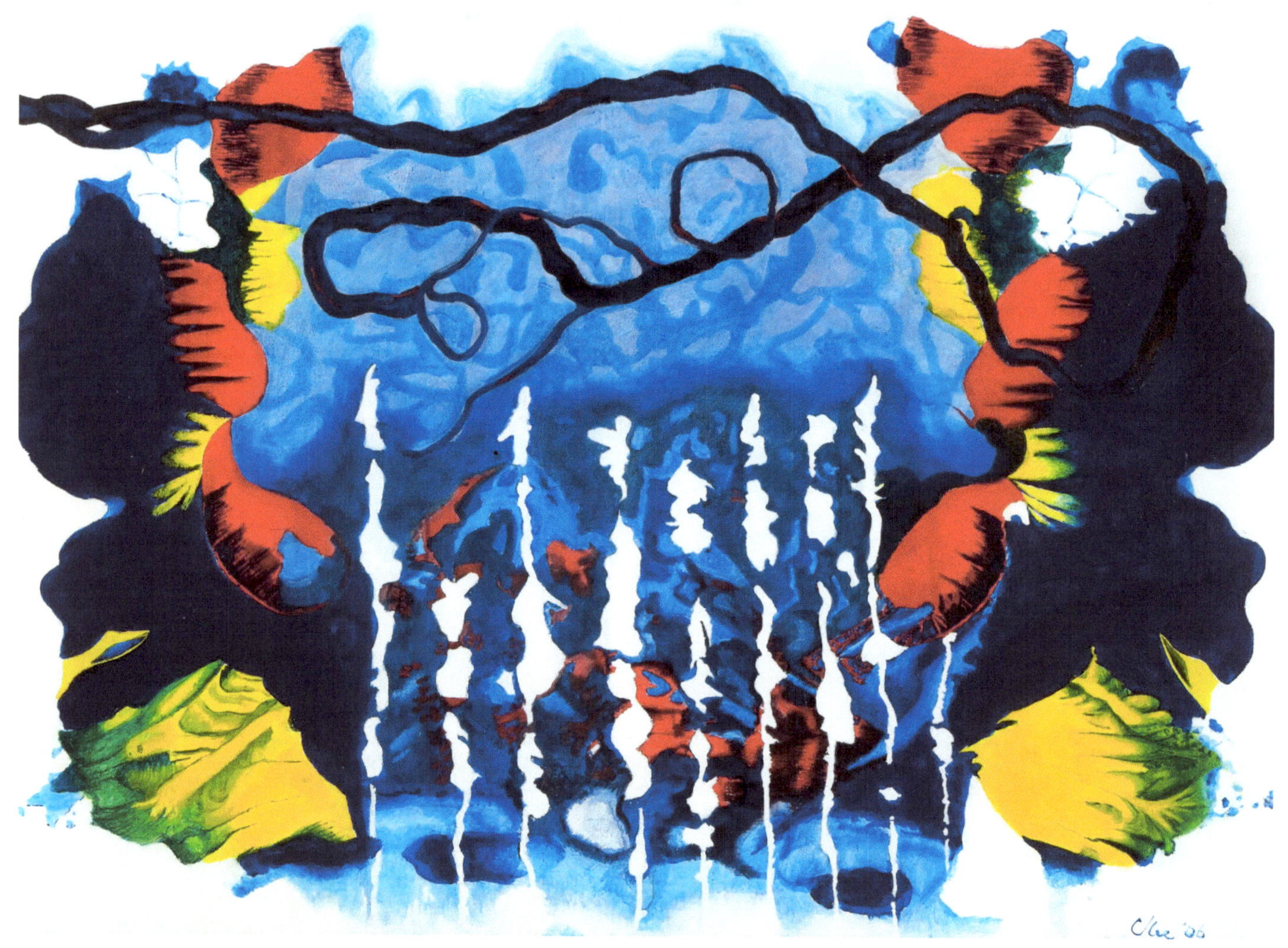

24 Years Old, Marriage

We had the same goal: to continue to study in Europe. He wanted to study in France and I was dreaming to go and study in Germany. We got married in Hawaii and began to study and have ambitions. I decided to study a different field "Interior Architecture". I enjoyed all the paintings and drawings. In this painting we see two people looking through a window into the indefinite and hopeful future.

Acrylic on Canvas 40x30 inch

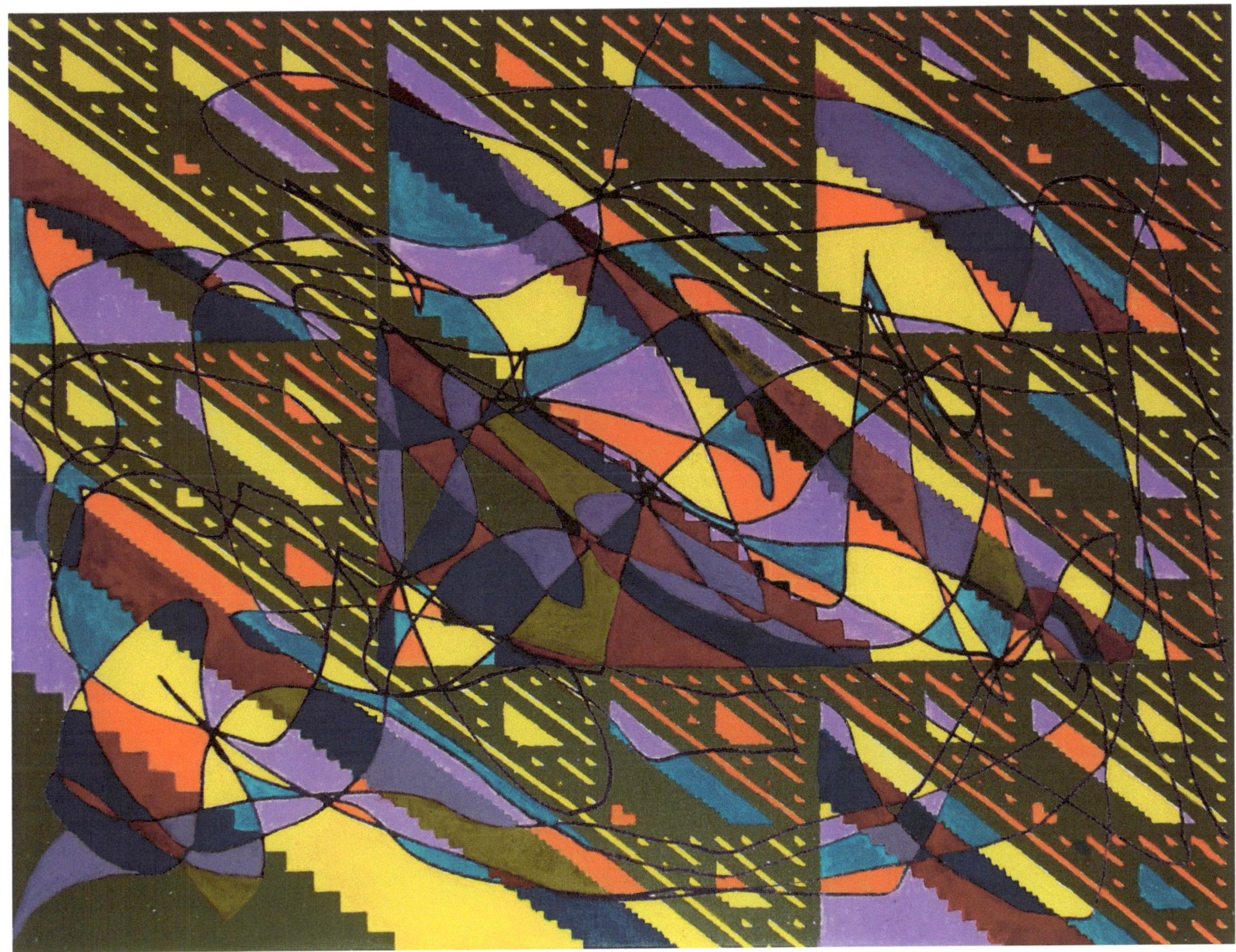

25 Years Old, Colorado

We decided to plan to study for two years in Paris France. First, we wanted to enjoy living in Colorado for a couple of months before we go to Europe. The majestic scale of the mountains in Colorado and the wonderful forests are so beautiful and provide challenging hiking. This painting conjures up the jagged mountains, rivers, and forests. We enjoyed hiking and camping all over the mountains.

Acrylic on Canvas 40x30 inch

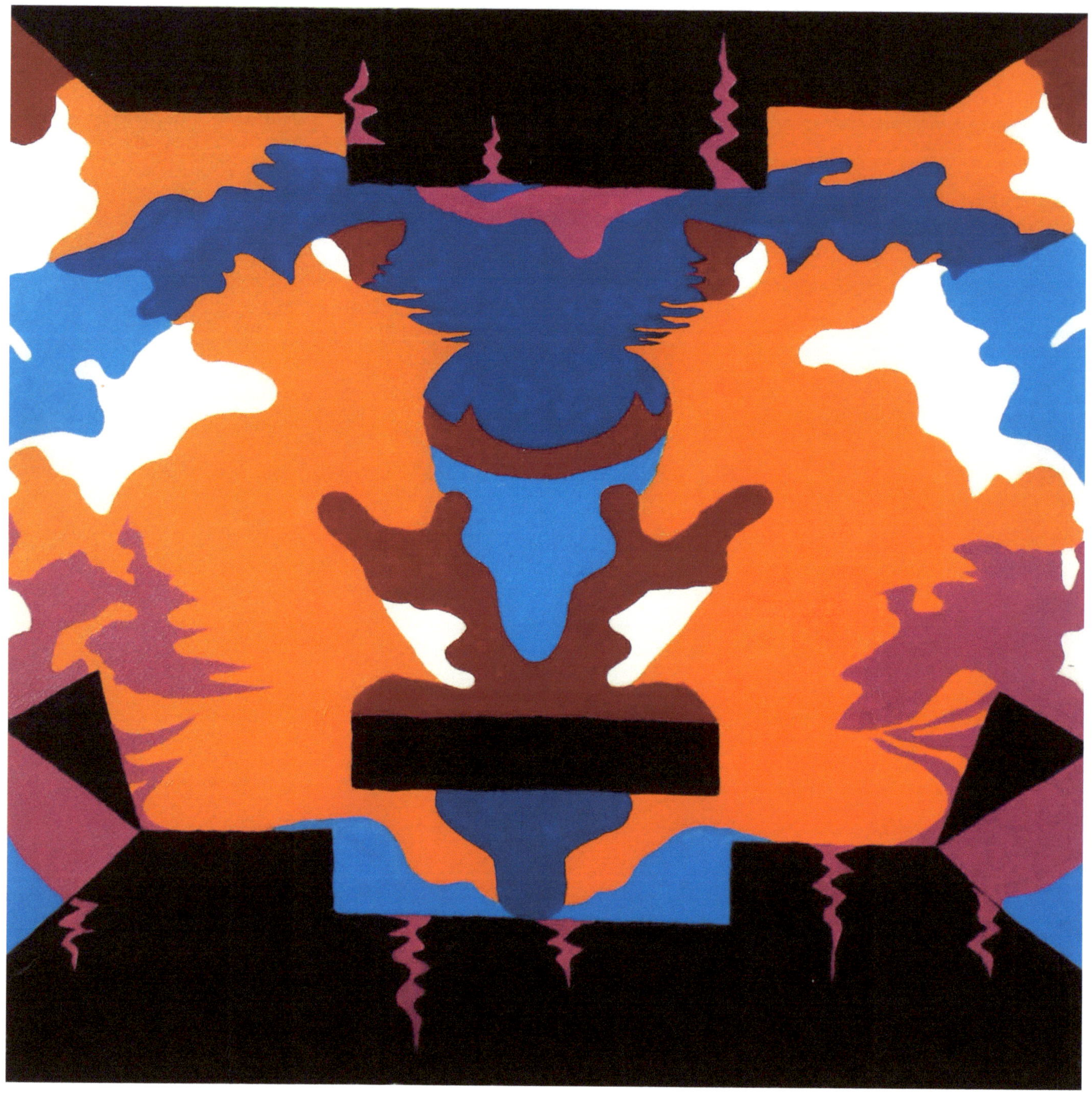

26 Years Old, Study in France

I started to study interior architecture in France. Everything was new and interesting to me. I was trying to know the French culture as deeply as possible. Learning the French language was also fun. The screws can go into another culture as deeply as possible and join life's experiences, like in this painting. It is very interesting to know and be part of other cultures.

Acrylic on Canvas 36x36 inch

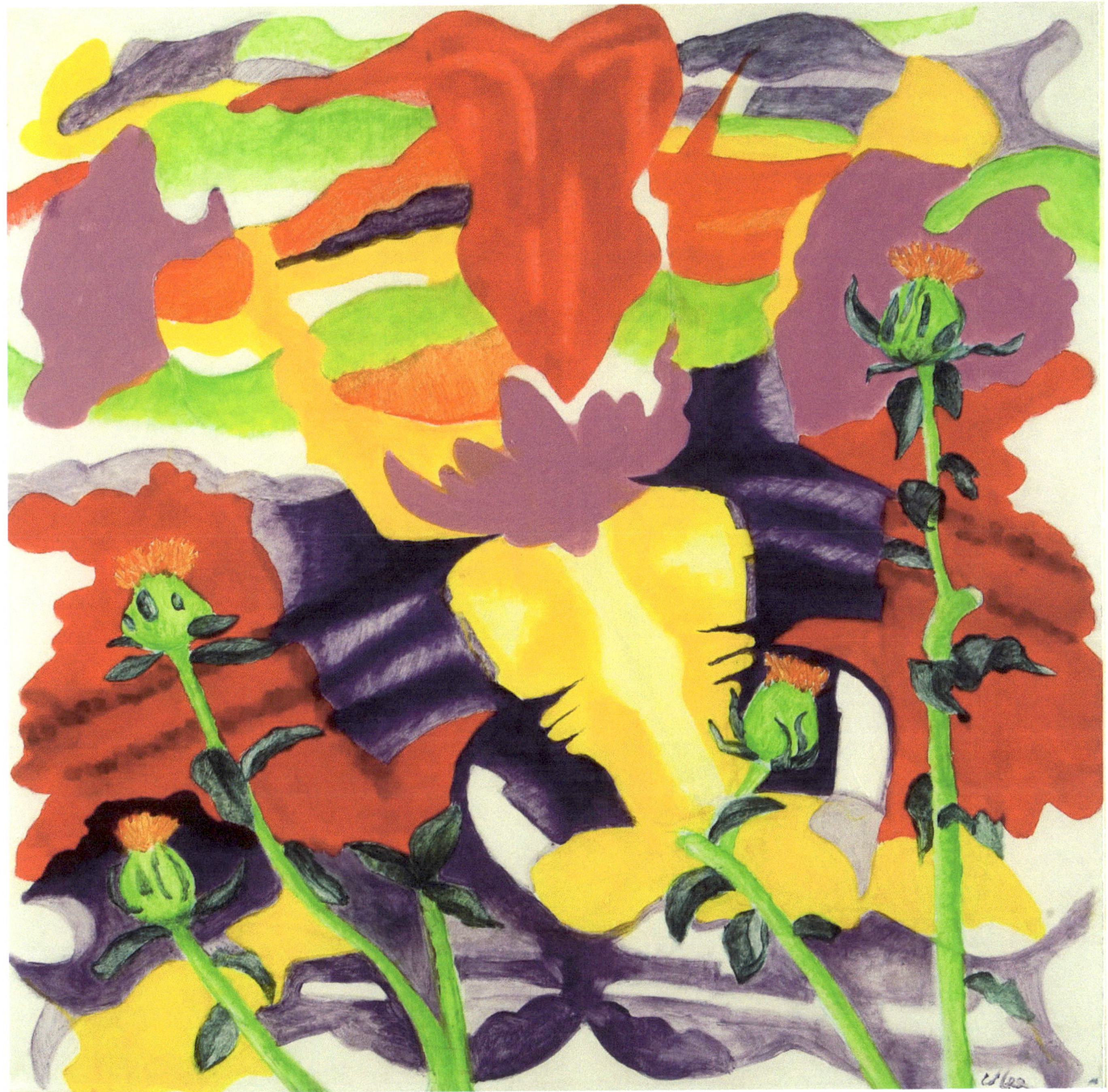

27 Years Old, Study in Paris

Paris is a wonderful and charming place for an artist. All the architecture is so beautiful and historic. The City gives beautiful vistas everywhere you go and everywhere you turn. Every single detail is designed with lots of care. All the different people are also impressive and put me in a happy mood. It is a joy to meet them and get to know them.

Acrylic on Canvas 36x36 inch

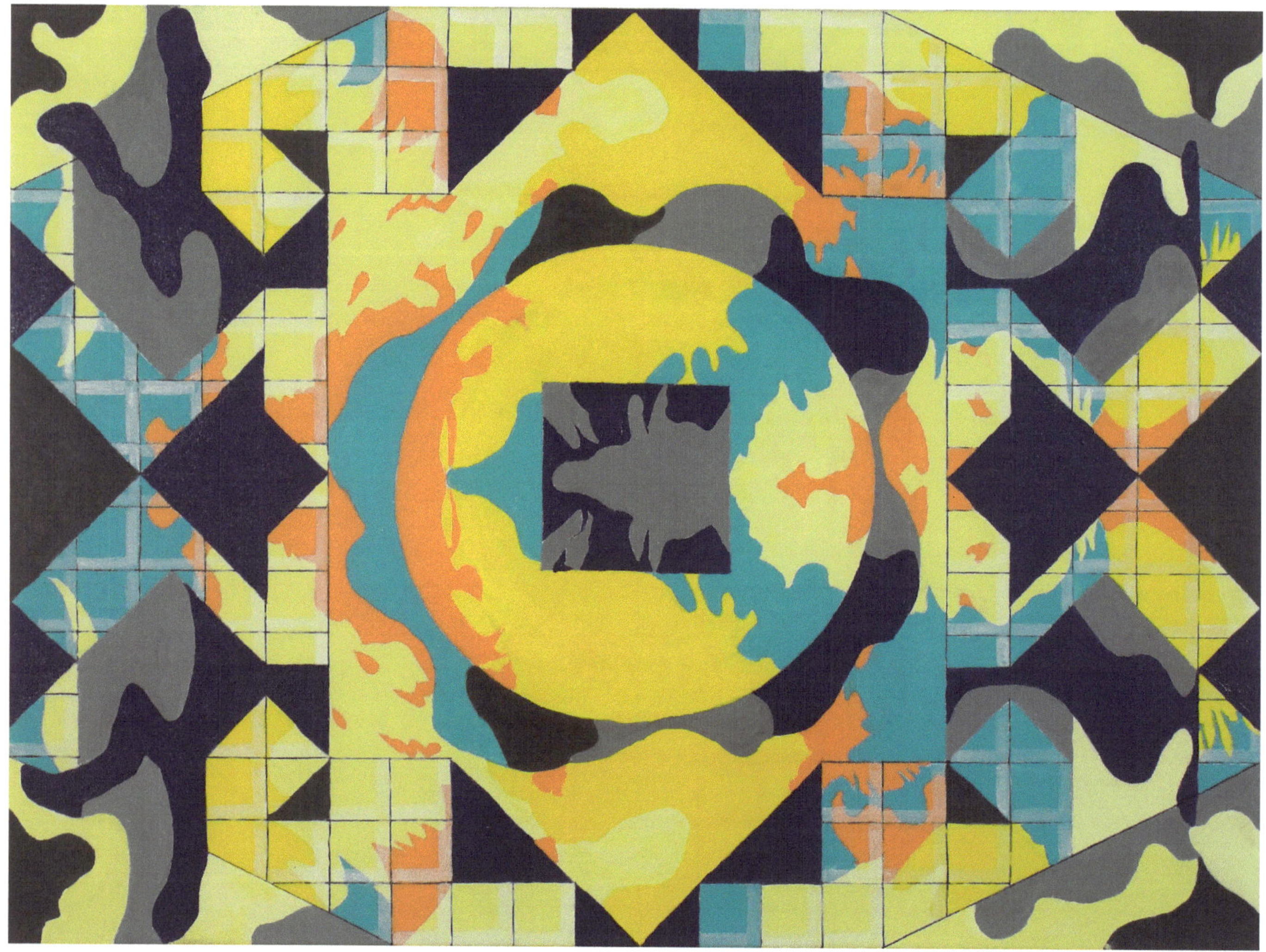

28 Years Old, Parson's and Geometry

I studied at Parson's School of Design in New York City. It was very hard because the way of teaching was so different from that in France and Korea. Geometry is the base of everything. To read geometry is to understand the language of the foundation of design. In this painting, we began to understand the complexity of the interaction of geometry and design. The ability to analyze the basic concepts of the design is a fundamental beginning to developing new designs.

Acrylic on Canvas 48x36 inch

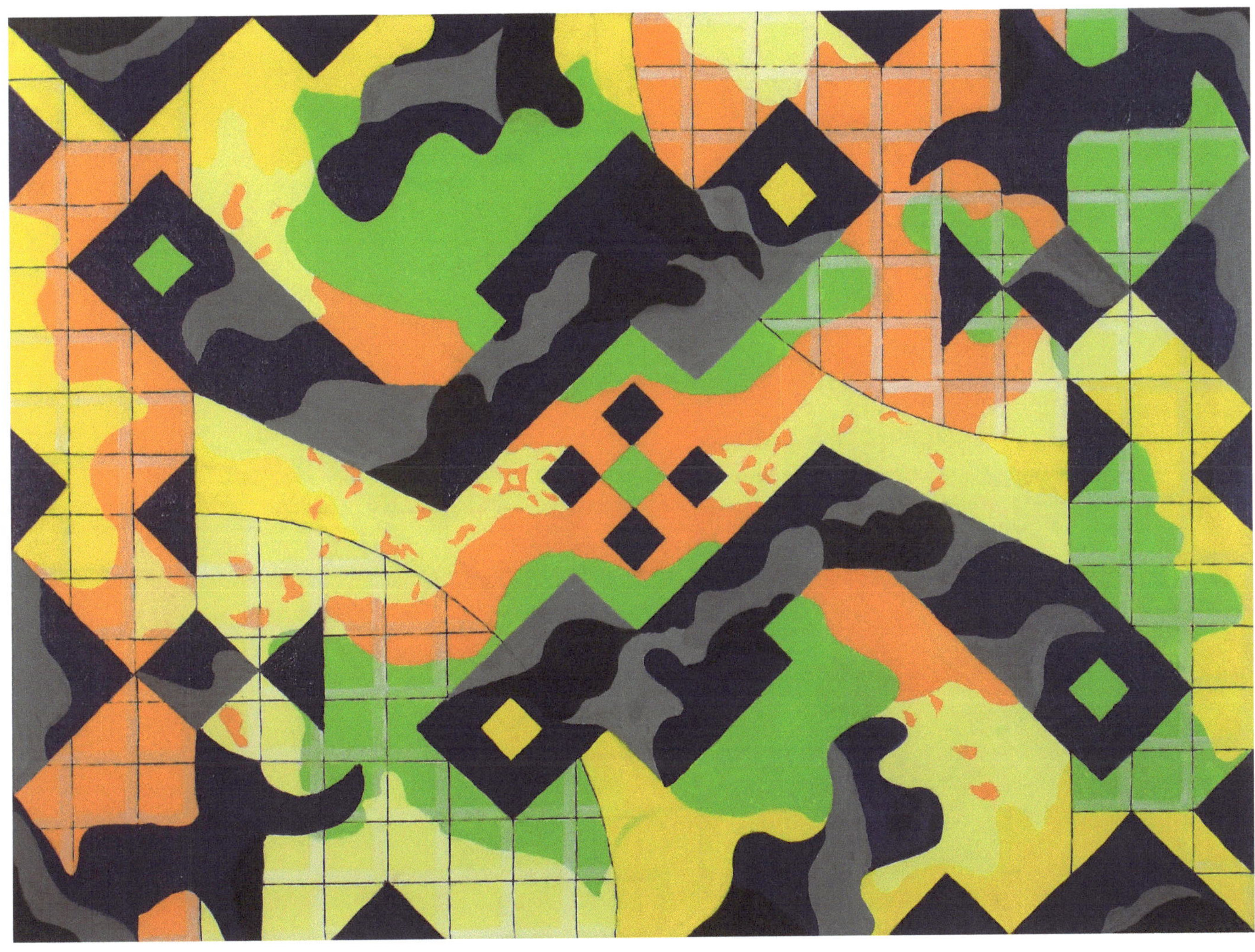

29 Years Old, Parson's and Architecture

Architecture is the mother of functional art. All the basics of art are combined to create functional designs. Philosophically nature is the beginning of architecture. Humans are from nature in the beginning. The aesthetics of the material and mathematical harmony is combined together. As you can see in this painting the proportions are a critical element of the overall design.

Acrylic on Canvas 48x36 inch

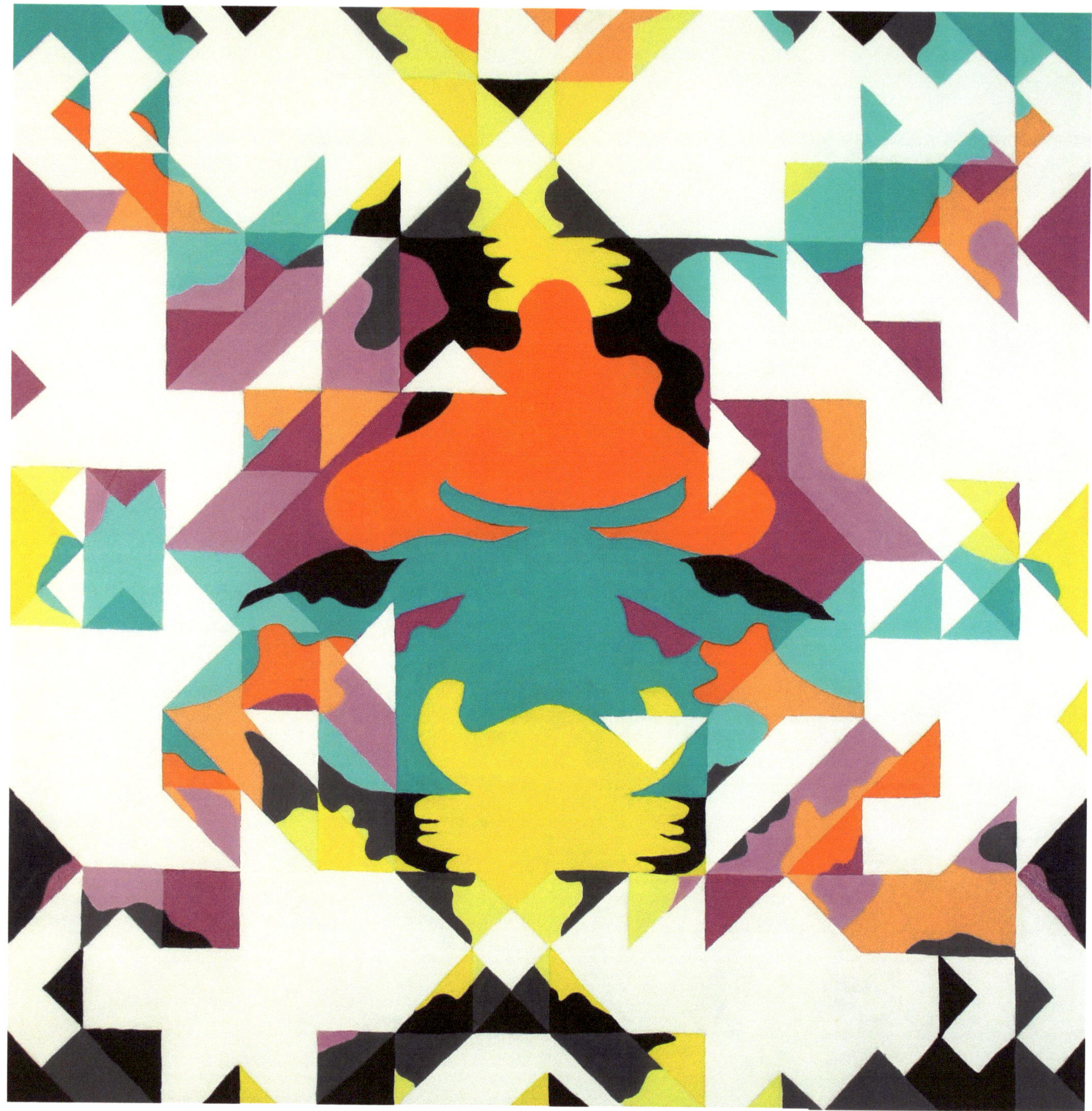

30 Years Old, Working at SOM

It was very colorful and fun to work with a lot of talented architects and designers. The projects are very interesting. The sharp contrast between good design and mediocre design is obvious and depends on the type of project. The forms and colors are very prominent and evolving. Architecture projects are always evolving.

Acrylic on Canvas 36x36 inch

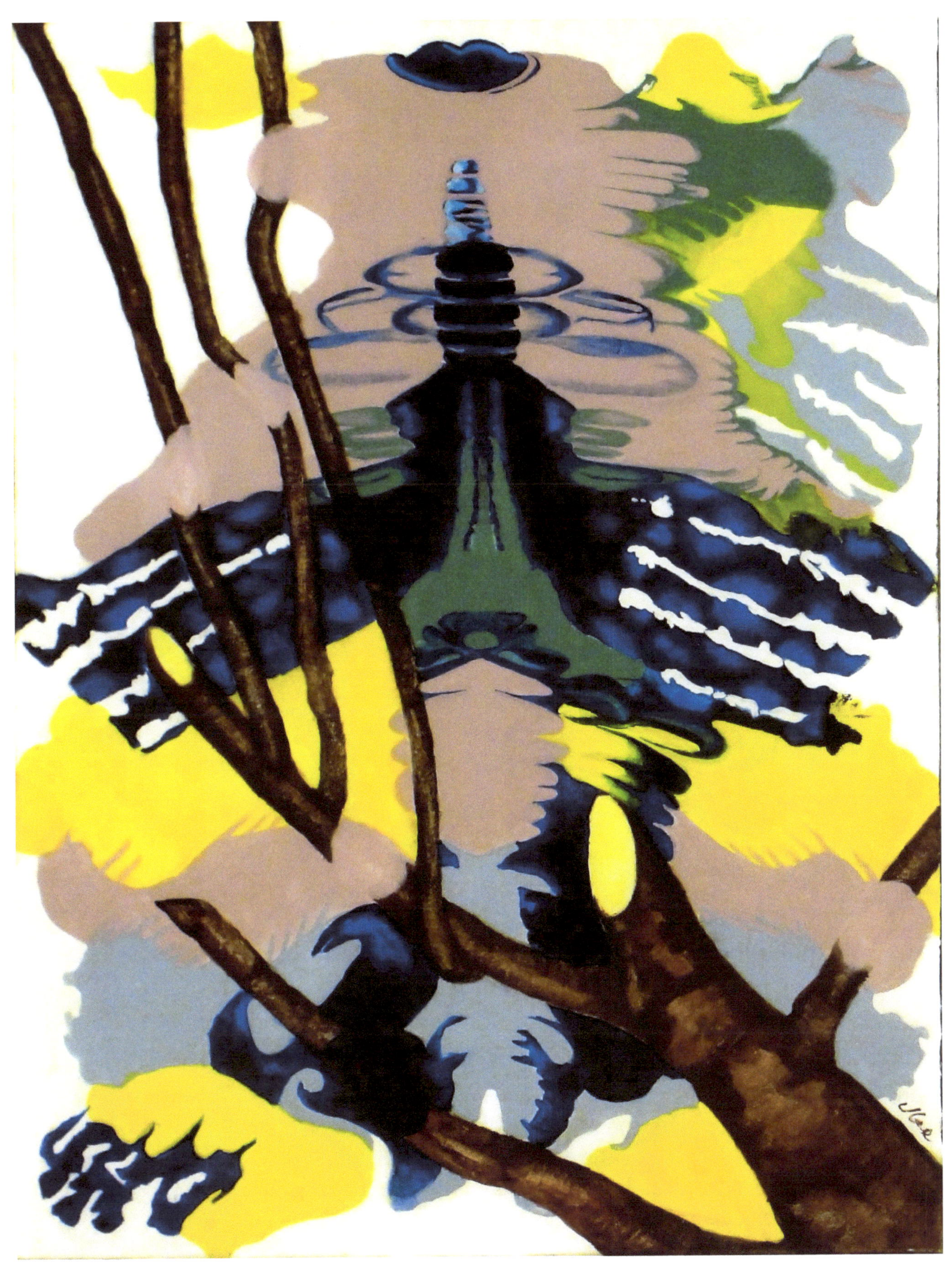

31 Years Old, Leaving SOM

Acrylic on Canvas 30x40 inch

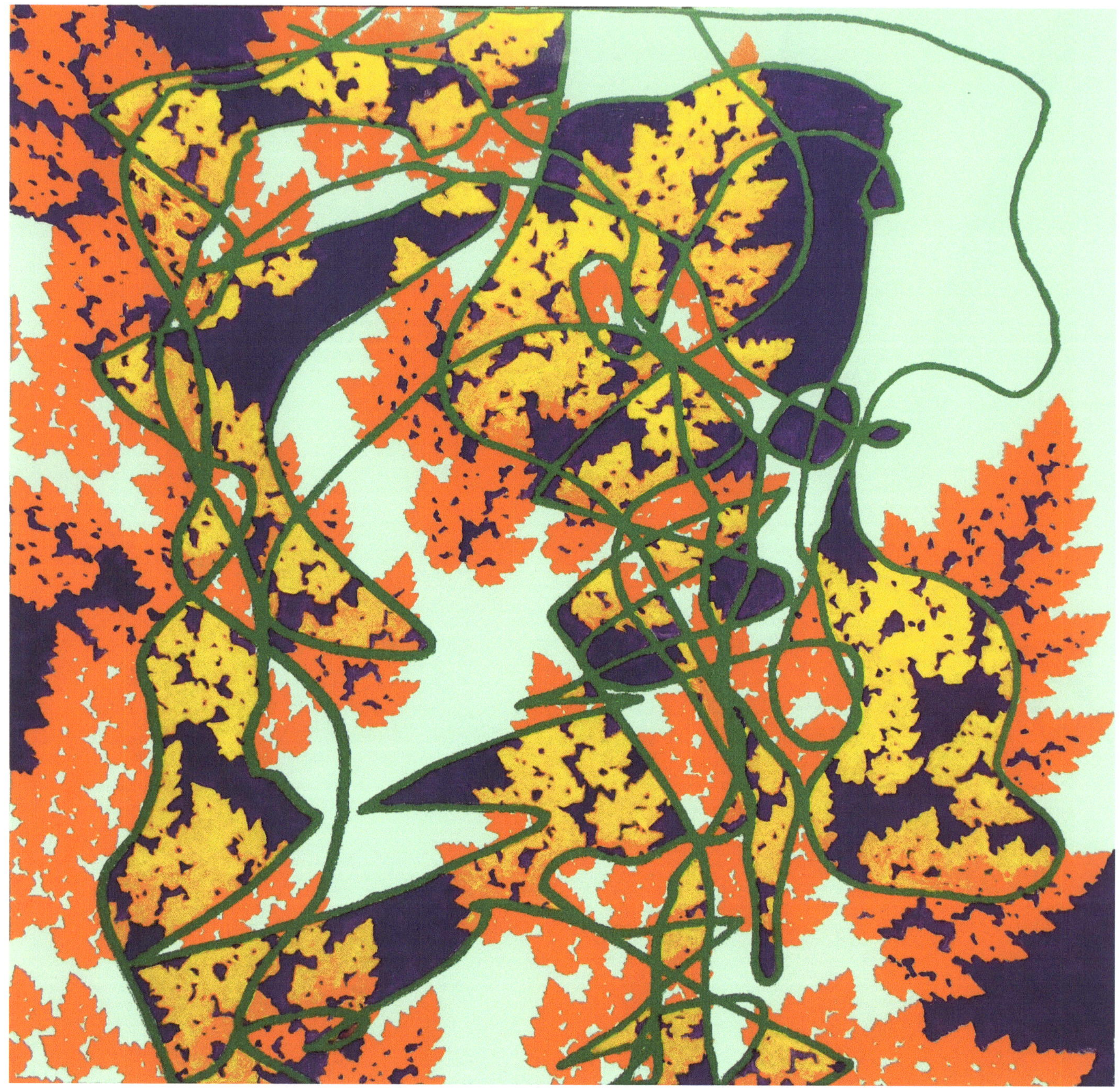

32 Years Old, Sailing

We are sailing in Long Island Sound every weekend in our boat "Ile d'Ouessent". We are most times on the water. It is not destination sailing just having fun. The trips to the small islands or swimming on their shores are beautiful. Sailing is like gliding through the autumn leaves. The grace of movement weaves us through the beautiful sailing paths.

Acrylic on Canvas 36x36 inch

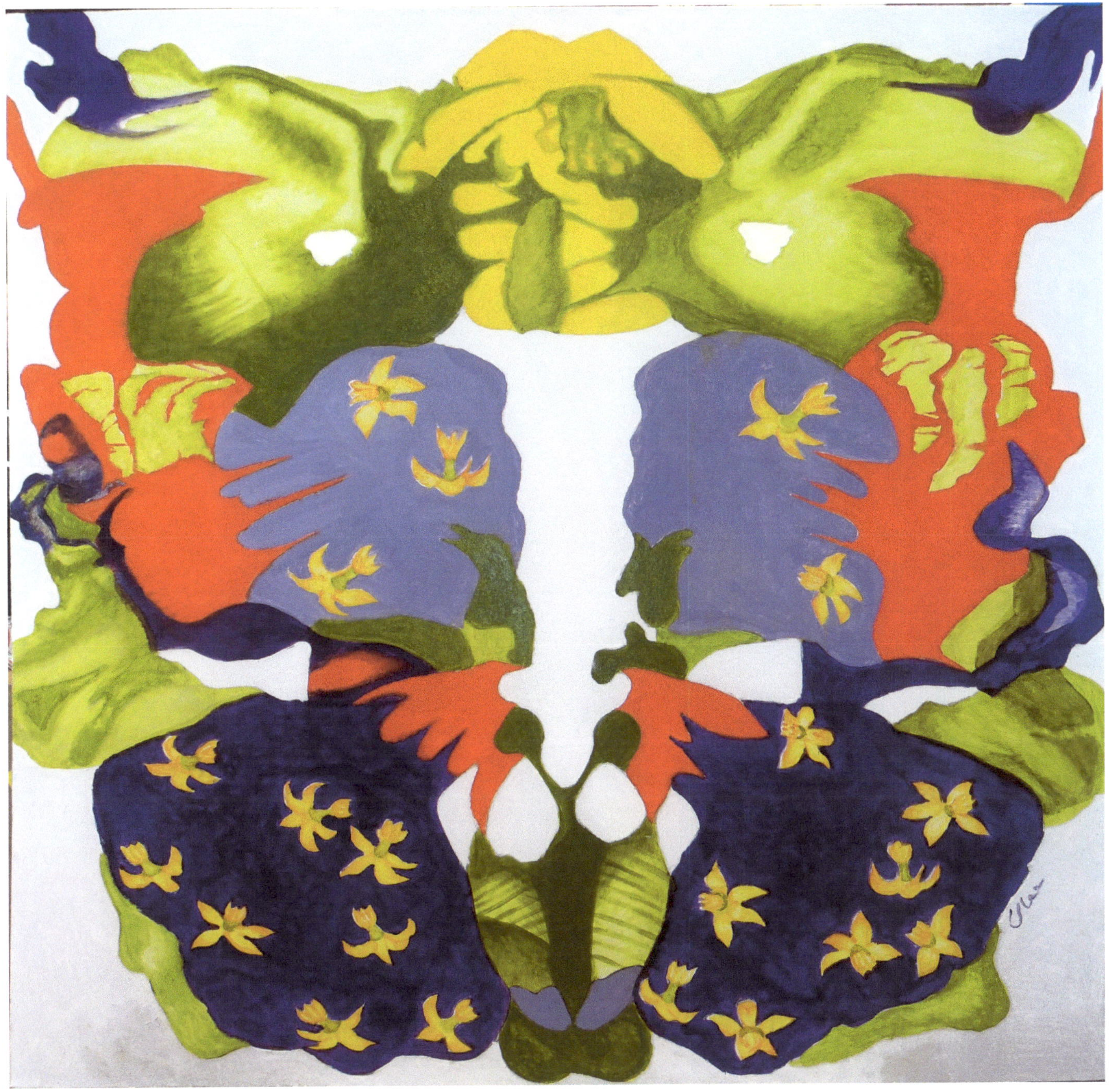

33 Years Old, My Own Design Company

I want to be my own boss. To develop my own ideas I need the freedom to express myself. The new concepts come from the beginning of freedom. I want to have my own design world and create my own space. My exploration of the mountains and nature are ready to be expressed in my Interior Designs for my clients.

Acrylic on Canvas 48x48 inch

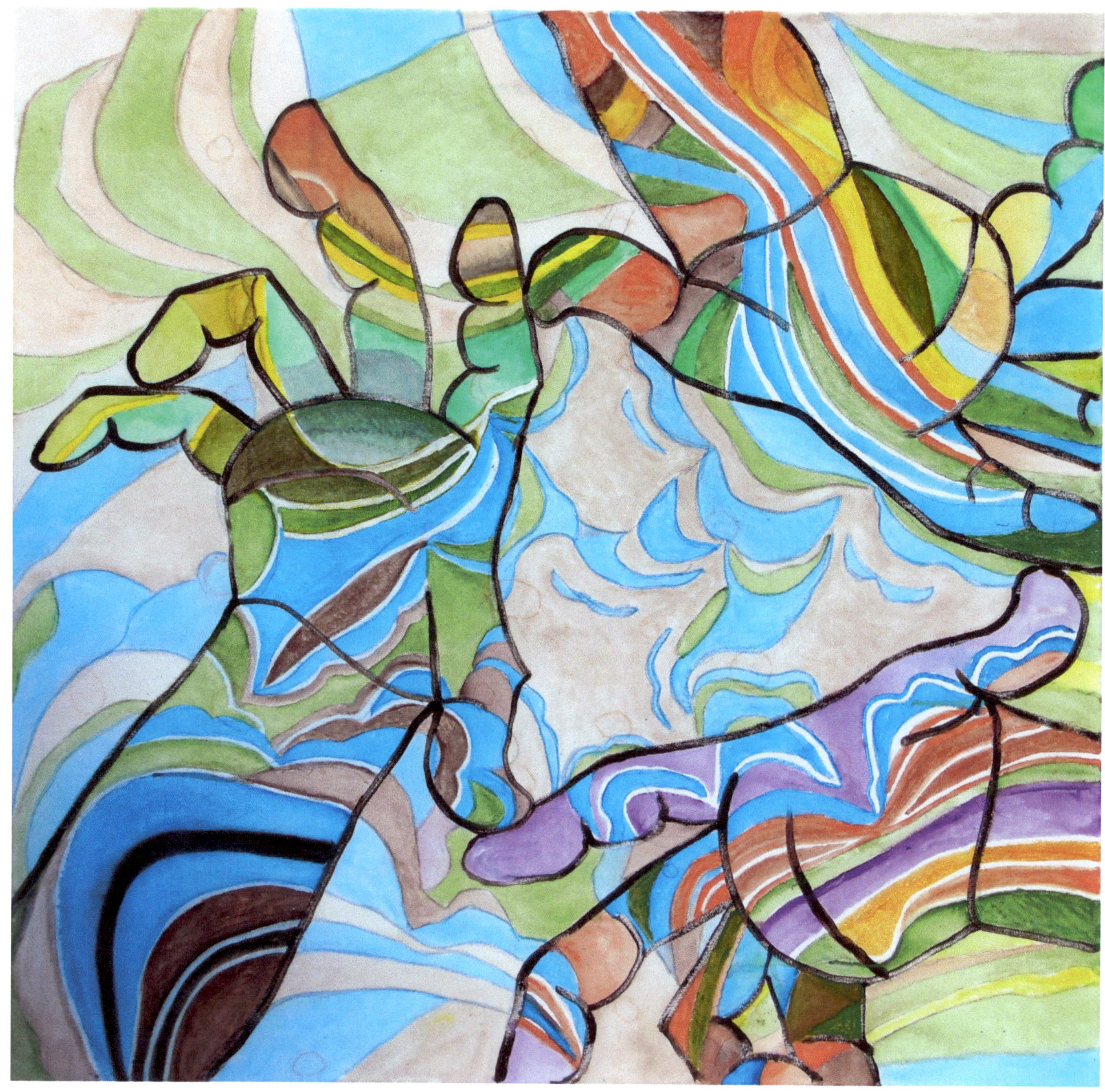

34 Years Old, ULJA

U. Lee-Johnson and Associates! It has been my dream to have my own Company. I could put my own stamp on my projects. It is not easy to run a Company. Especially where Art and managing are combined. I was always ambitious about my projects. I could control everything with my own hands. It is hard to balance periods of too much work and too little work.

Acrylic on Canvas 36x36 inch

Chapter 4 – Pregnancy, Depression, Despair

I became a mother, the joy of being a parent and playing with my children filled me with happiness. My life dream was continuing but then came depression.

After the birth of Adam I hit a major depression. The depression was severe and associated with schizophrenia. I required medical intervention and was hospitalized. Hospital was a terrible and frightening experience. At this time I separated from my husband, lost custody of my child and divorced.

My life was broken, no career, no child, no marriage, everything fell apart.

Recovery was difficult. Not having a my own family and being unable to care for myself I moved in with my sister. She supported me and helped me recover sufficiently to again live by myself in New York City.

I was alone. I was taking strong medication that had serious side effects that caused me to sleep a lot. My life had collapsed.

I started painting and sculpting at the Art Students League in New York City. Slowly I recovered, made new friends and got great solace in my art. My art saved my life.

I had to support myself and returned to Interior Design and worked for Companies in New York City. The spark and enthusiasm had gone. I was no longer a lead designer and visionary and found the work boring and tedious but I needed to support myself.

I started to travel again and very slowly my life began to develop in a new direction.

The paintings in this chapter cover years 35 through 49 and cover my depression and slow recovery.

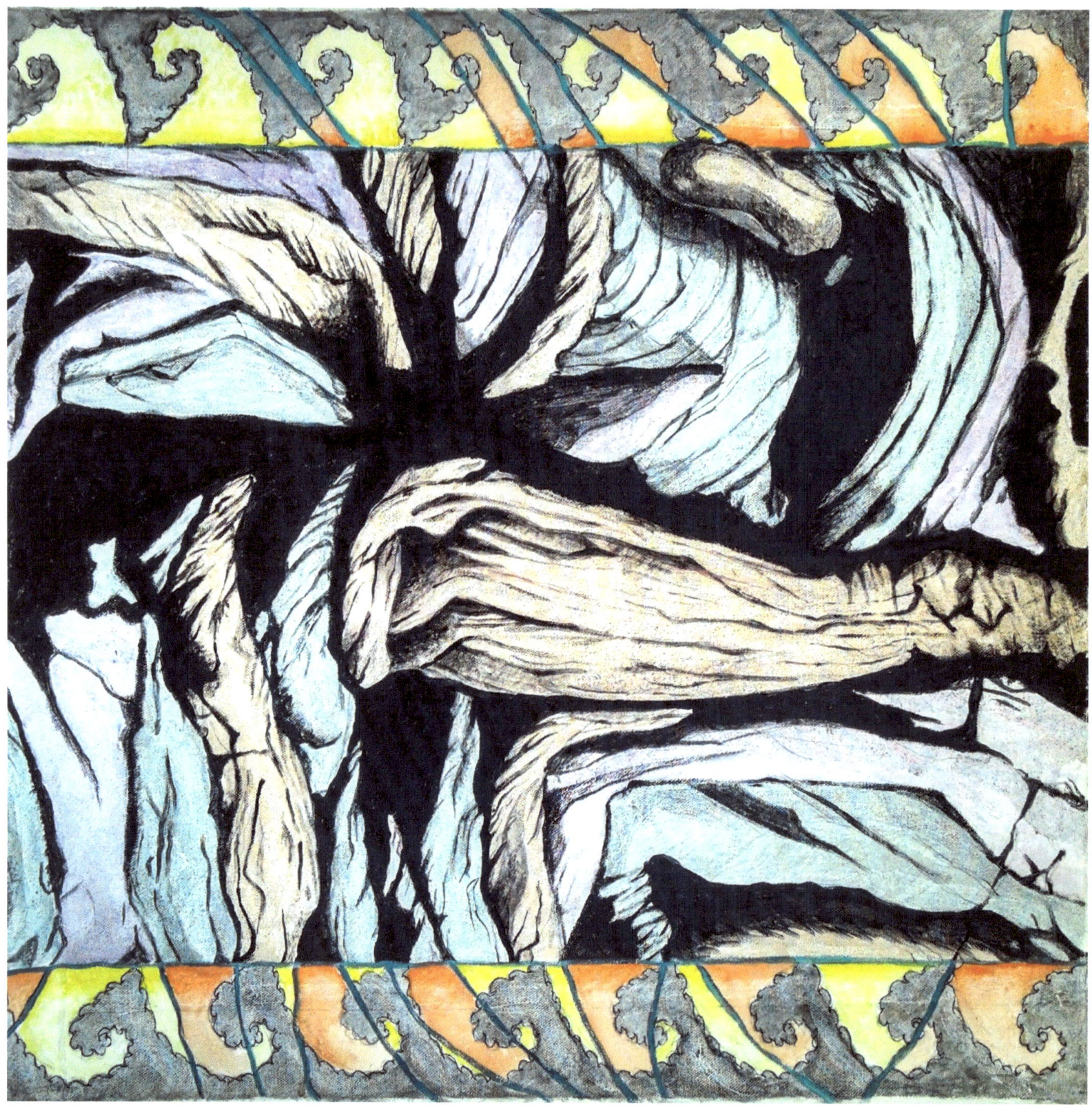

35 Years Old, Pregnancy

The time of pregnancy is planned. Considering career and having a baby and life with a child. The child will develop over time into a complex human character. Time can also create natural fractal elements. In the development of a coastline, the fractal is created as time erodes and ruptures the earth's surface. The longer the time the geography becomes more toned and balanced. In this painting, the pregnant earth creates lava that is born. The lava is eroded and is the child that is formed by nature creating the complex land, mountains, and rivers.

Acrylic on Canvas 24x24 inch

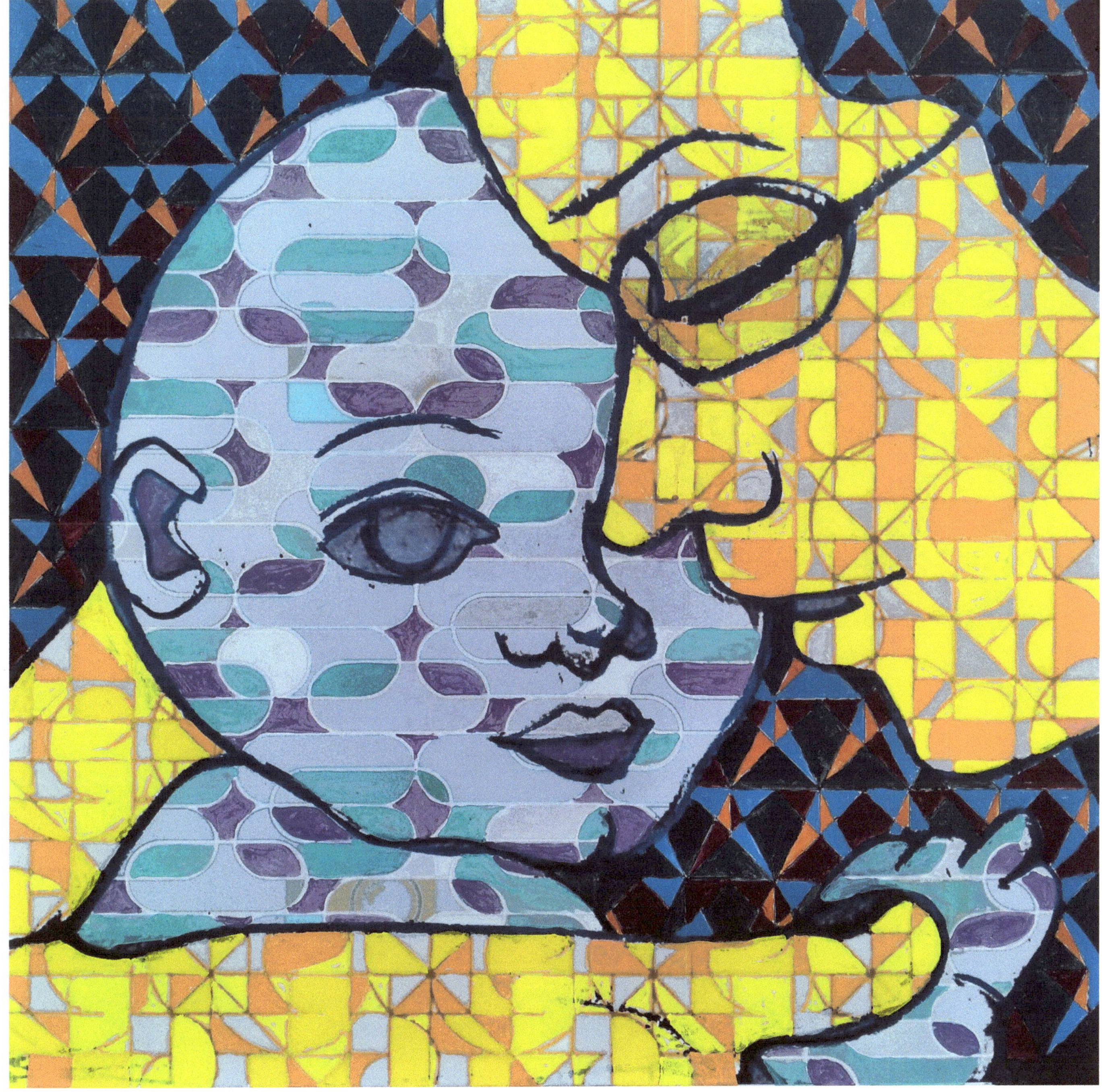

36 Years Old, Baby Adam

The baby Adam is a pleasure to be with. As a baby, he seems to understand his surroundings well. He does not cry often without reason. It is one of the most beautiful times of all. I always give him a beautiful hug. It is such a fulfilling moment. This painting shows the feeling of the moment and that is something I will cherish all my life.

Acrylic on Canvas 39x39 inch

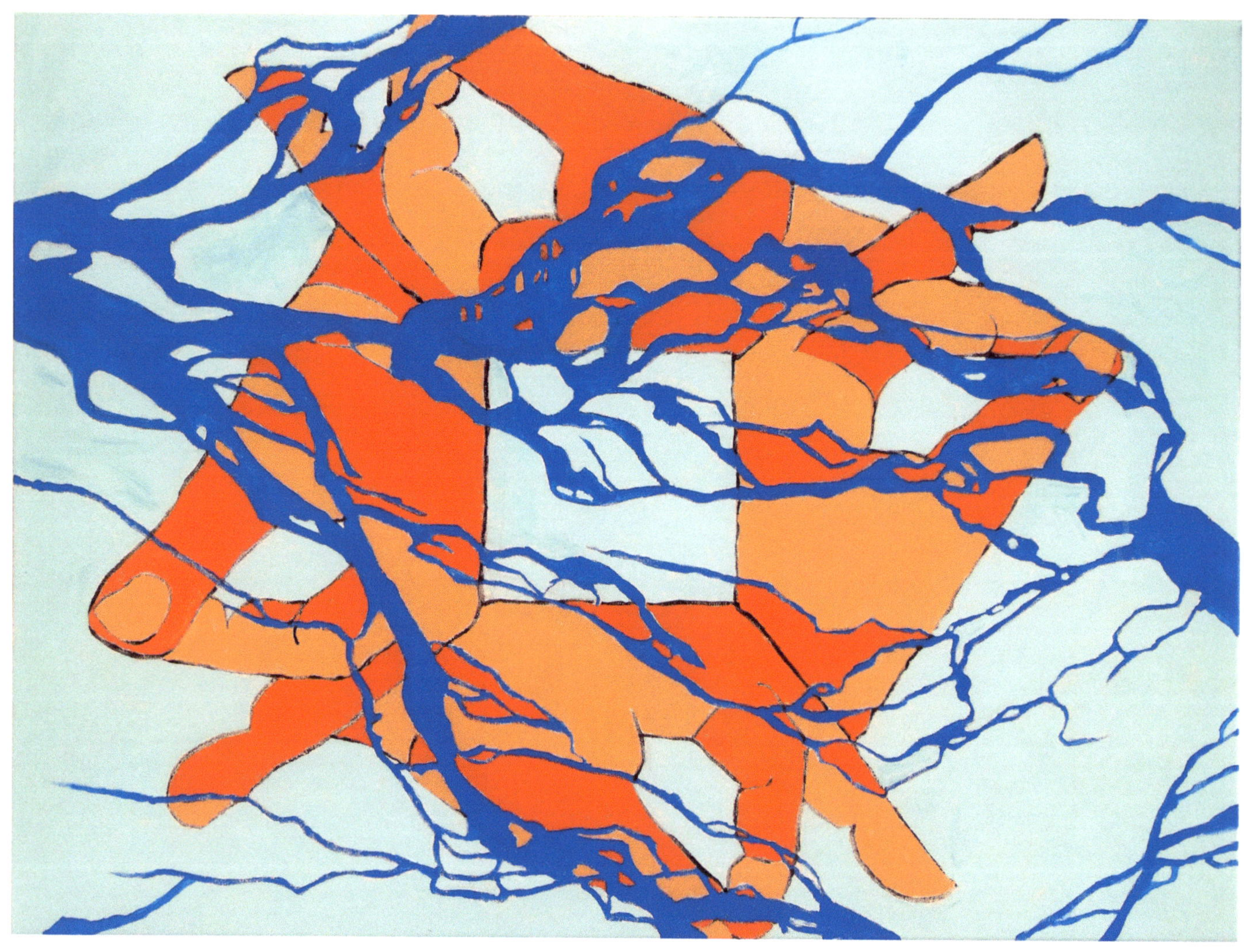

37 Years Old, Growing Adam

Adam is growing up as a beautiful baby. He does not cry often at all. We went sailing overnight with a neighbor couple, one of whom was a medical doctor, who thought Adam was developing wonderfully. He is multiplying in all different directions like a fractal movement. The fractal winding river is like a new life exploring multiple possibilities and makes a beautiful composition about new life and future hopes.

Acrylic on Canvas 40x30 inch

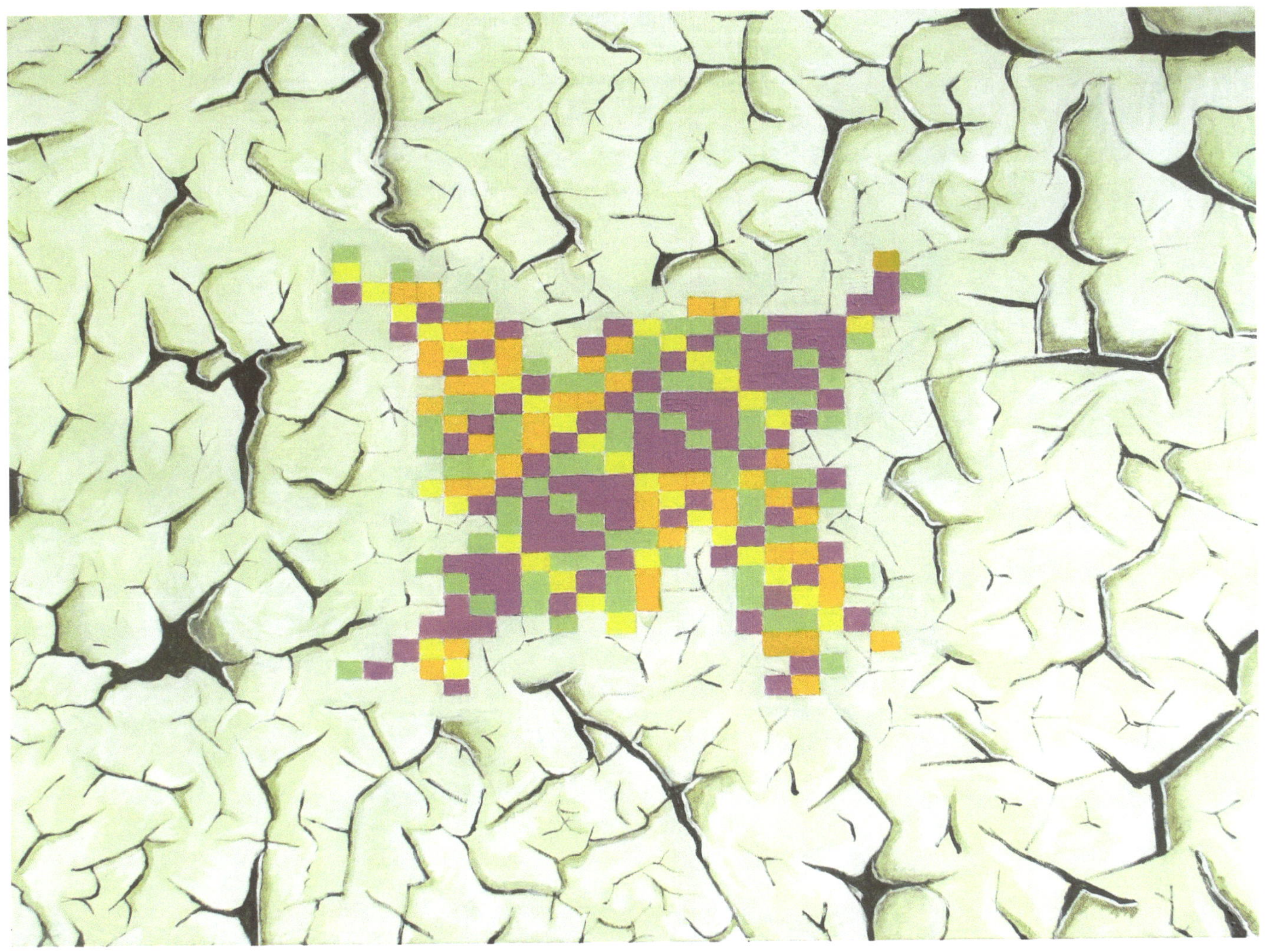

38 Years Old, Broken Life!

Life can be broken apart sometimes. A crack will open more and more. Cracks are complex fractal shapes representing the multitude of interactions in life. The fractal elements indicate the progression of life and evolving situations. Fractals are self-similar shapes small cracks growing on larger cracks, like in life small problems grow into and fragment larger problems into complex situations. My life started to have cracks and openings. The openings are fractal and evolve into bigger and bigger gaps and unresolved developments.

Acrylic on Canvas 40x30 inch

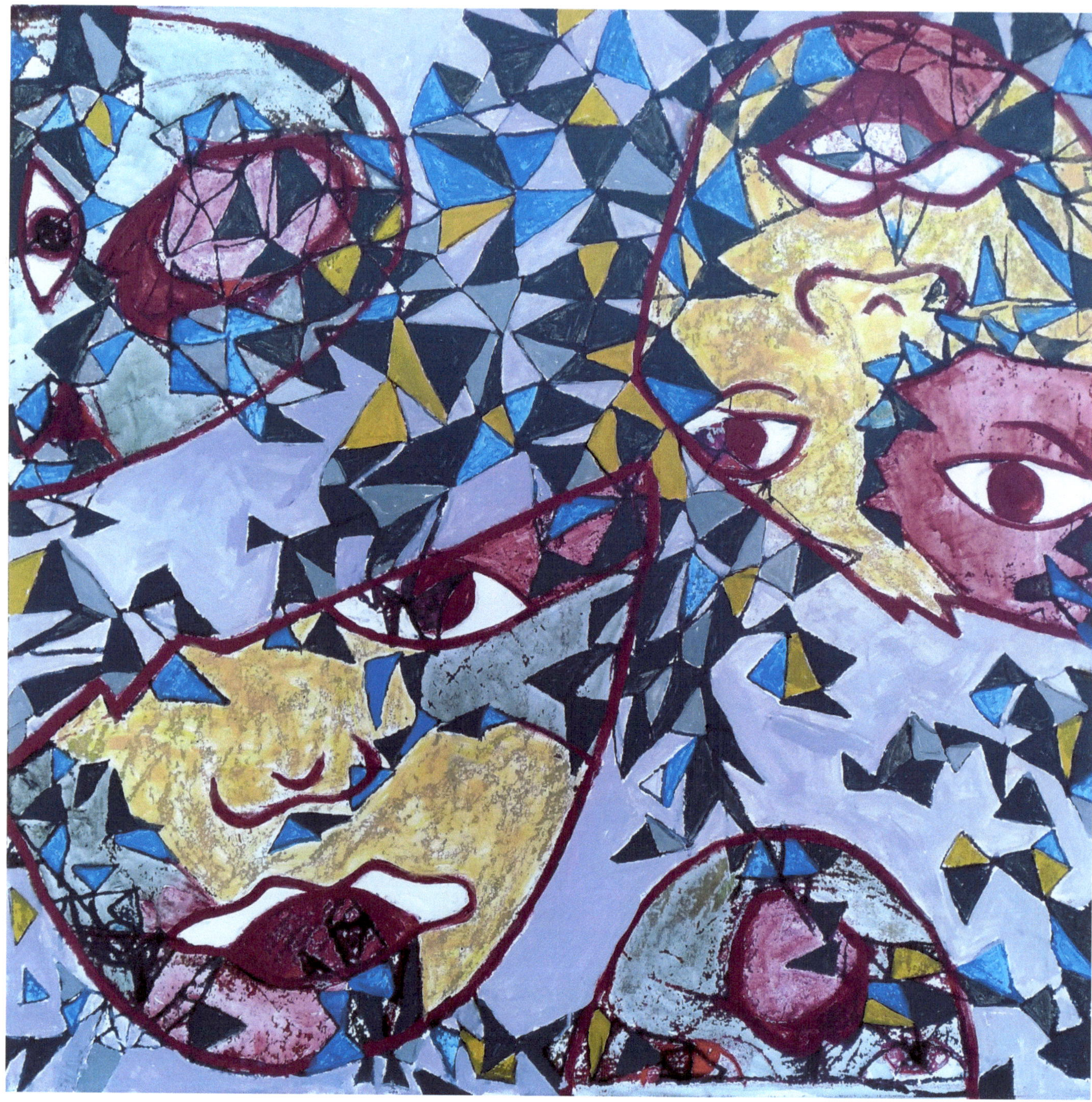

39 Years Old, Separation

Our marriage separation is imminent. There remains a little bit of hope but negative feelings are dominant. We are going to go our separate ways and see how the future will develop. Even though I am initiating the separation it is a very painful moment in my life. My two sisters are very shocked and lose themselves. This painting shows my mixed-up feelings and the external emotions of my husband and two sisters.

Acrylic on Canvas 39x39 inch

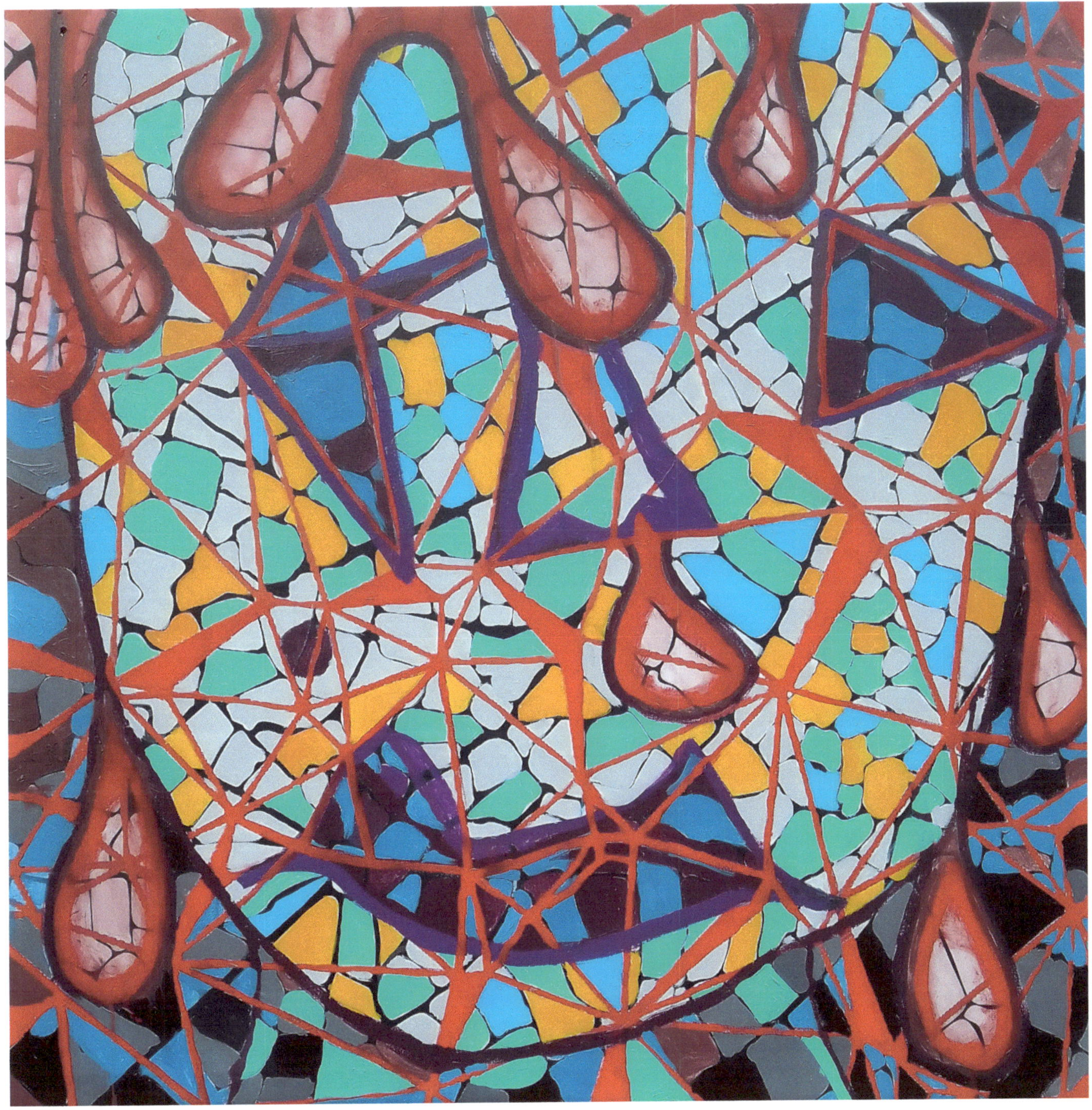

40 Years Old, In Hospital

I have been hospitalized due to major depression. I had started taking antidepressants after the pregnancy. I stopped taking the medication regularly and had a big depressive episode. Because of the hospitalization, I lost custody of my son. I did not know how to accept the situation at all. In this painting, I show the hospital as a very scary place with lots of different patients. I felt isolated and torn apart and treated like a nonhuman and a non-citizen.

Acrylic on Canvas 39x39 inch

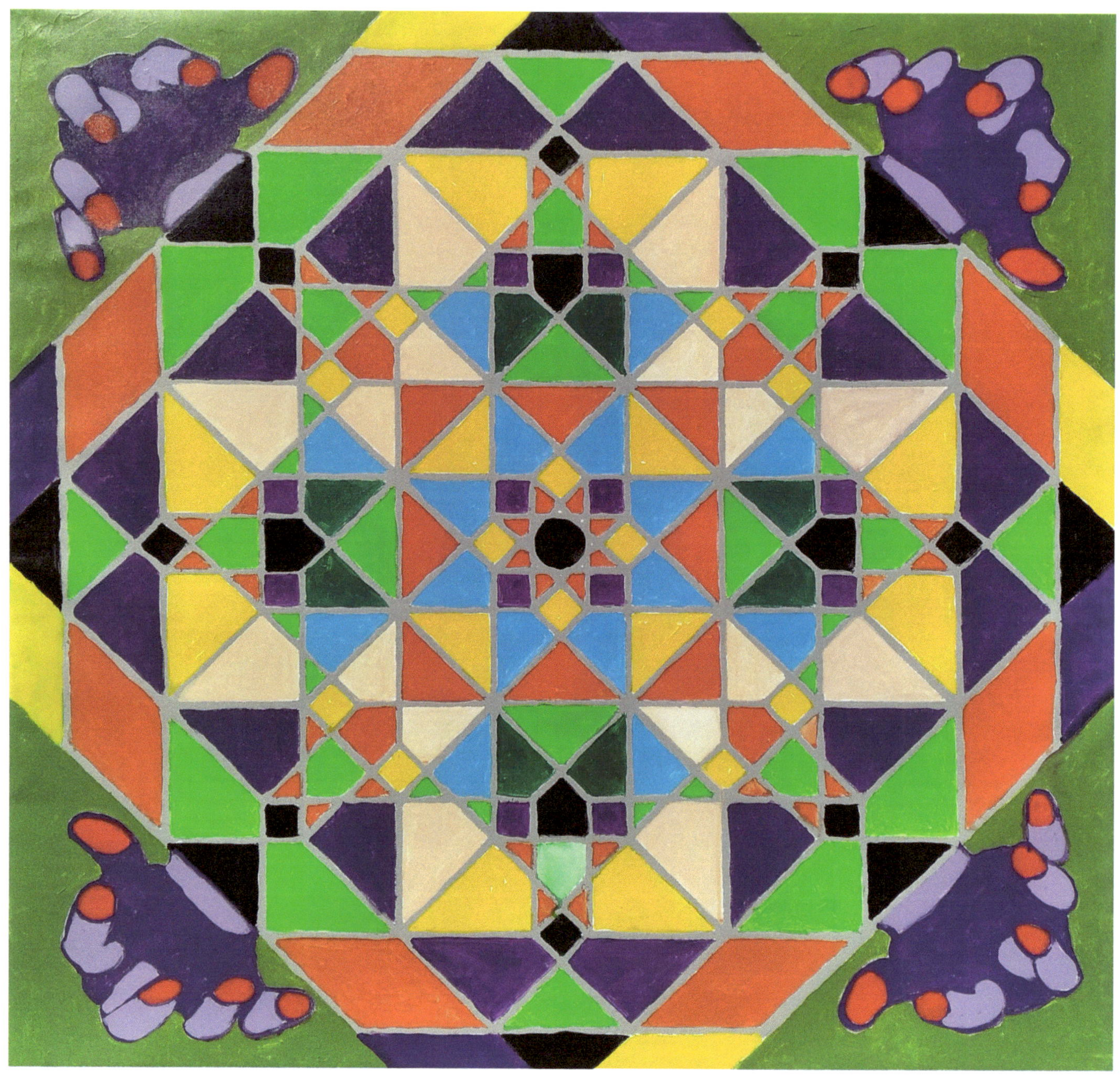

41 Years Old, My Sister's Home

I have been staying and being taken care of by my sister in Washington DC for about a year. It is very warm and bright after the hospital. However, I felt external threats about my divorce that I was not well enough to handle. I felt alone. I try to go with the flow of my sister's family. My sister has two daughters. I helped to take care of my nieces as best I could. I was getting better little by little and started doing voluntary work. I am grateful to my sister's family forever for helping my recovery. In this painting, we see the brightness of the supporting family. However, in the corners, there are legal, financial, and social threats.

Acrylic on Canvas 40x40 inch

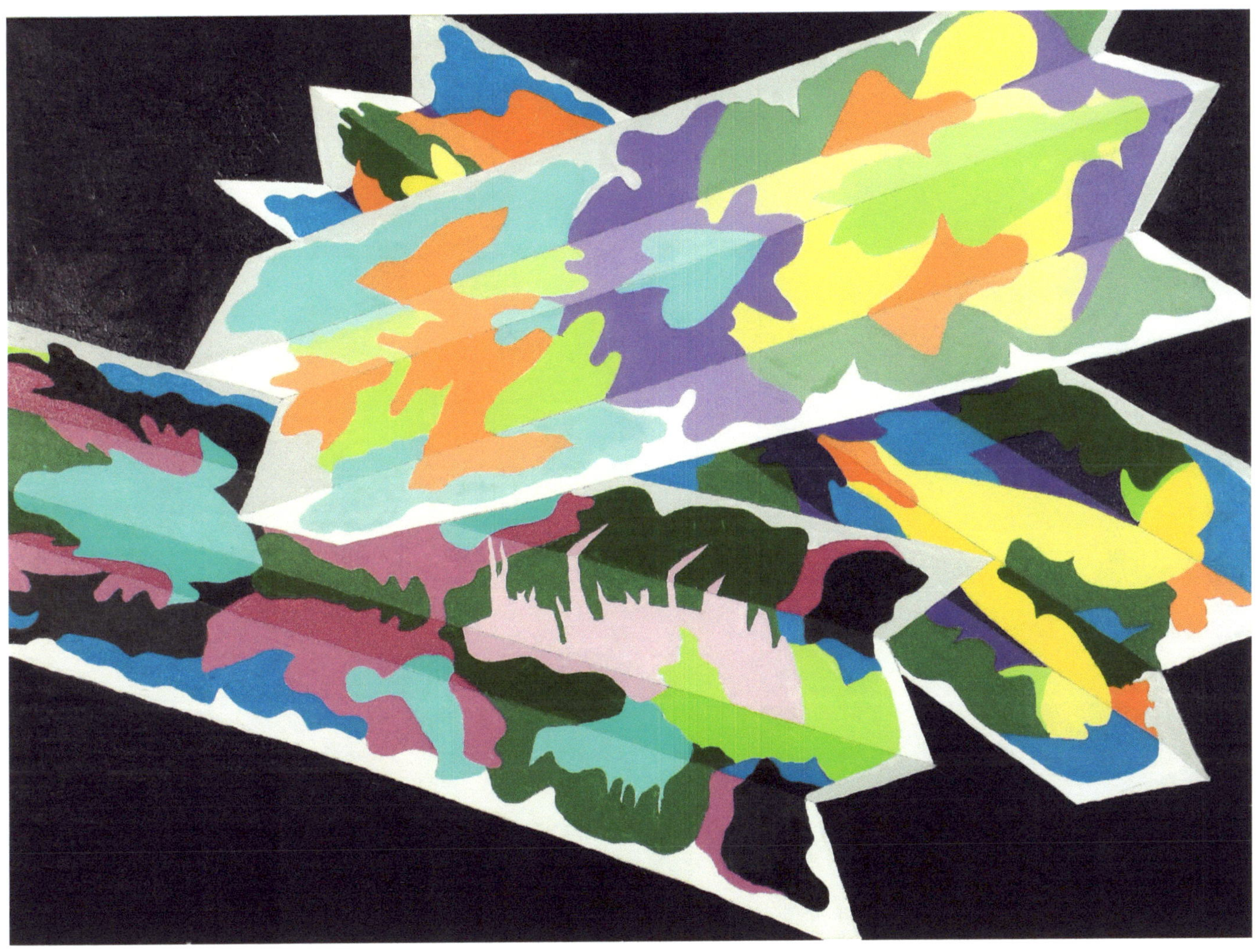

42 Years Old, Three Sisters

We three sisters do not agree on the same things Especially about my divorce. It is hard to go through this difficult period without family support. This is particularly true because of different cultures, The Korean way is to assimilate to the agreed feelings and opinions. I think that I have been at my most delicate and I have been the strongest at this time. Divorce is really hard. I have always been the strong one who sets life goals and works towards them. In this painting, the sharp edges and folds represent the relationship friction, yet the supportive soft feelings and colors are the most prominent. The strong dark opposite feelings are far away from me. Going through a divorce is one of the most difficult things in my life.

Acrylic on Canvas 40x30 inch

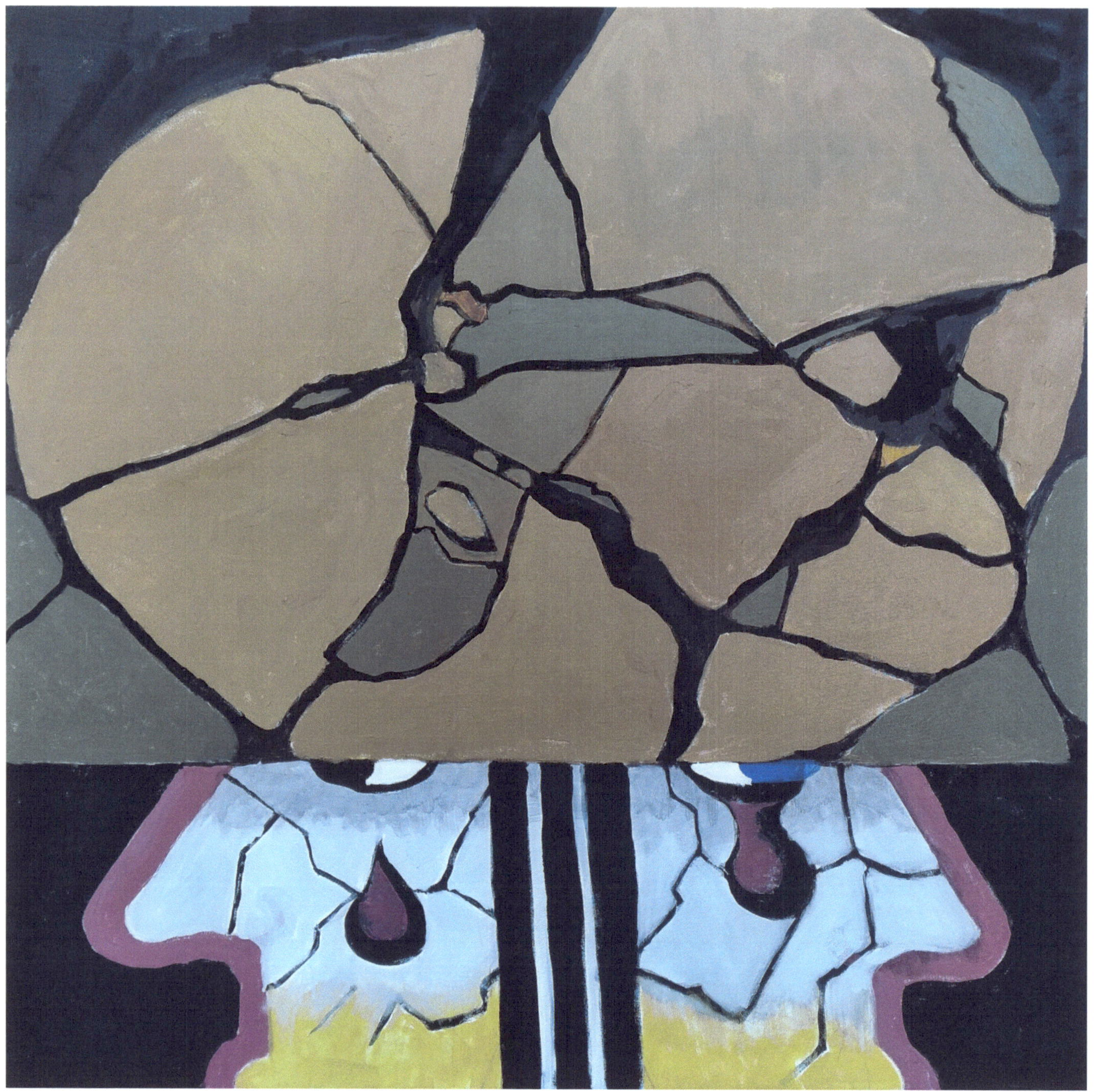

43 Years Old, Divorce

We are going through a divorce after three years of separation. It is better to think about the future and not the trouble and bad feelings of divorce. There is the inherent sadness of a life and relationship gone by. The breaking of the hard stone is followed by a lot of sadness. The sadness gets stronger when I think about our son Adam. It is very hard now but a sunny day will come. This painting illustrates the sadness, looking away and our minds turning into hard fractured bitter stone.

Acrylic on Canvas 39x39 inch

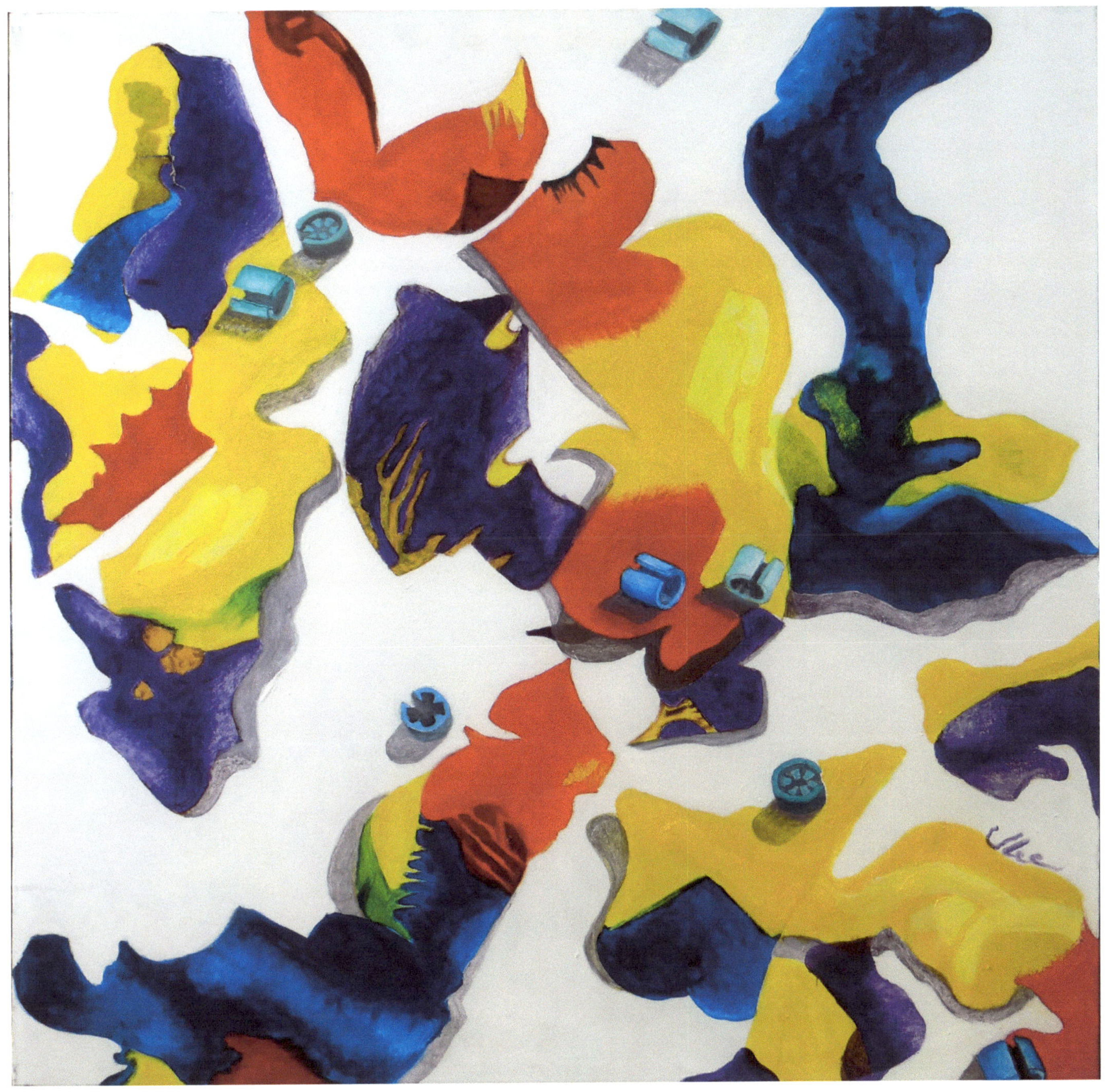

44 Years Old, Medication Side Effects

Because of the side effects of the medicine I am taking I could not work well and paint delicate things. I feel like I am floating in the air disconnected from reality. I am unable to settled down and concentrate. I was using simple materials like tearing paper and making a collages. This had the effect of helping me free myself and express creativity. This painting, not a collage, shows my fragmented and floating and disconnected feelings.

Acrylic on Canvas 36x36 inch

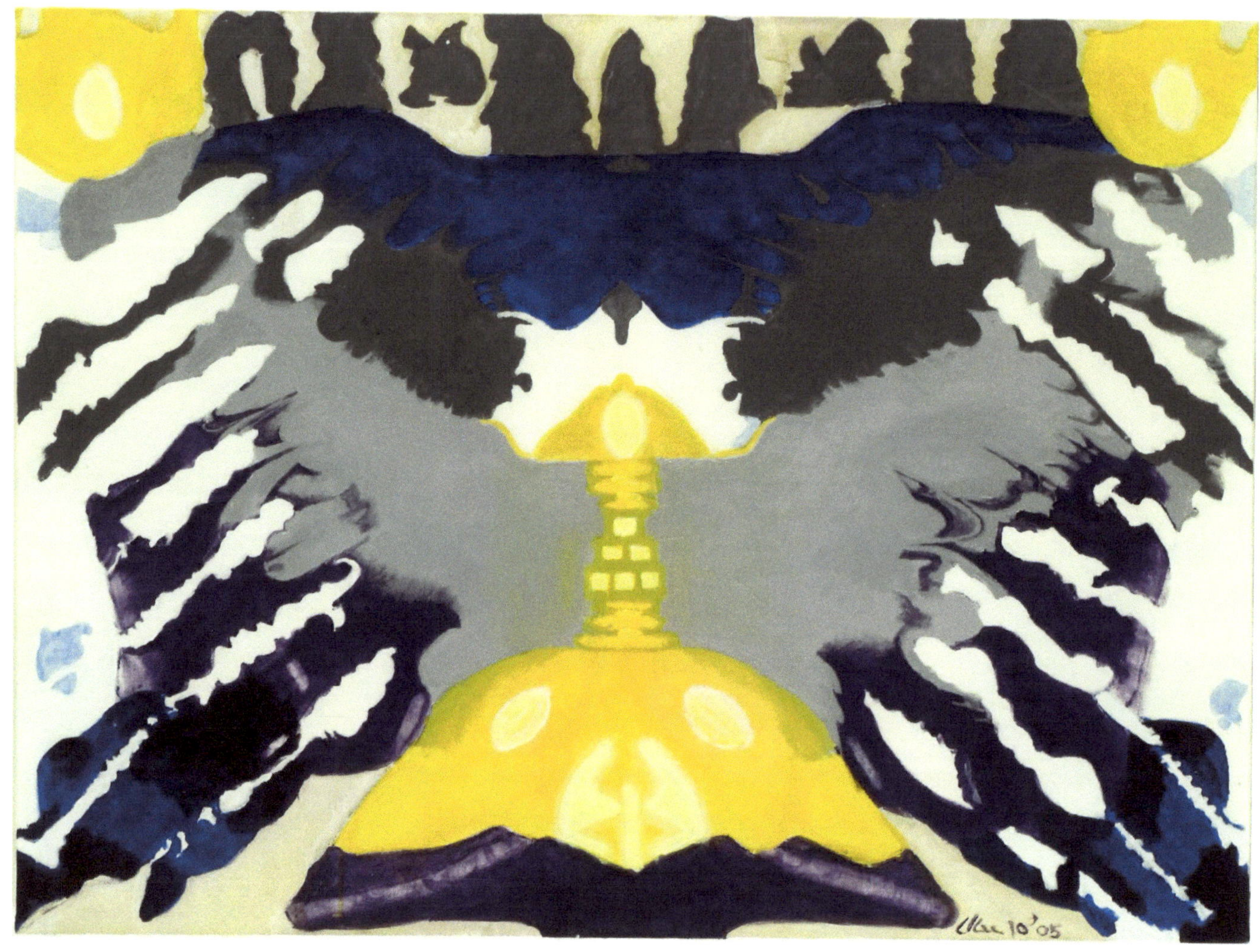

45 Years Old, Sleeping Side Effect

Taking antidepressant medicine is hard. I was knocked down by strong medicine. My doctor and I experimented with a variety of combinations, the side effects were I was sleeping until the afternoon. I could not accomplish much at this time which added to the depression the medicine was supposed to relieve. This painting conjures up the grey sleepy feeling always under the wings of tiredness and lack of energy.

Acrylic on Canvas 40x30 inch

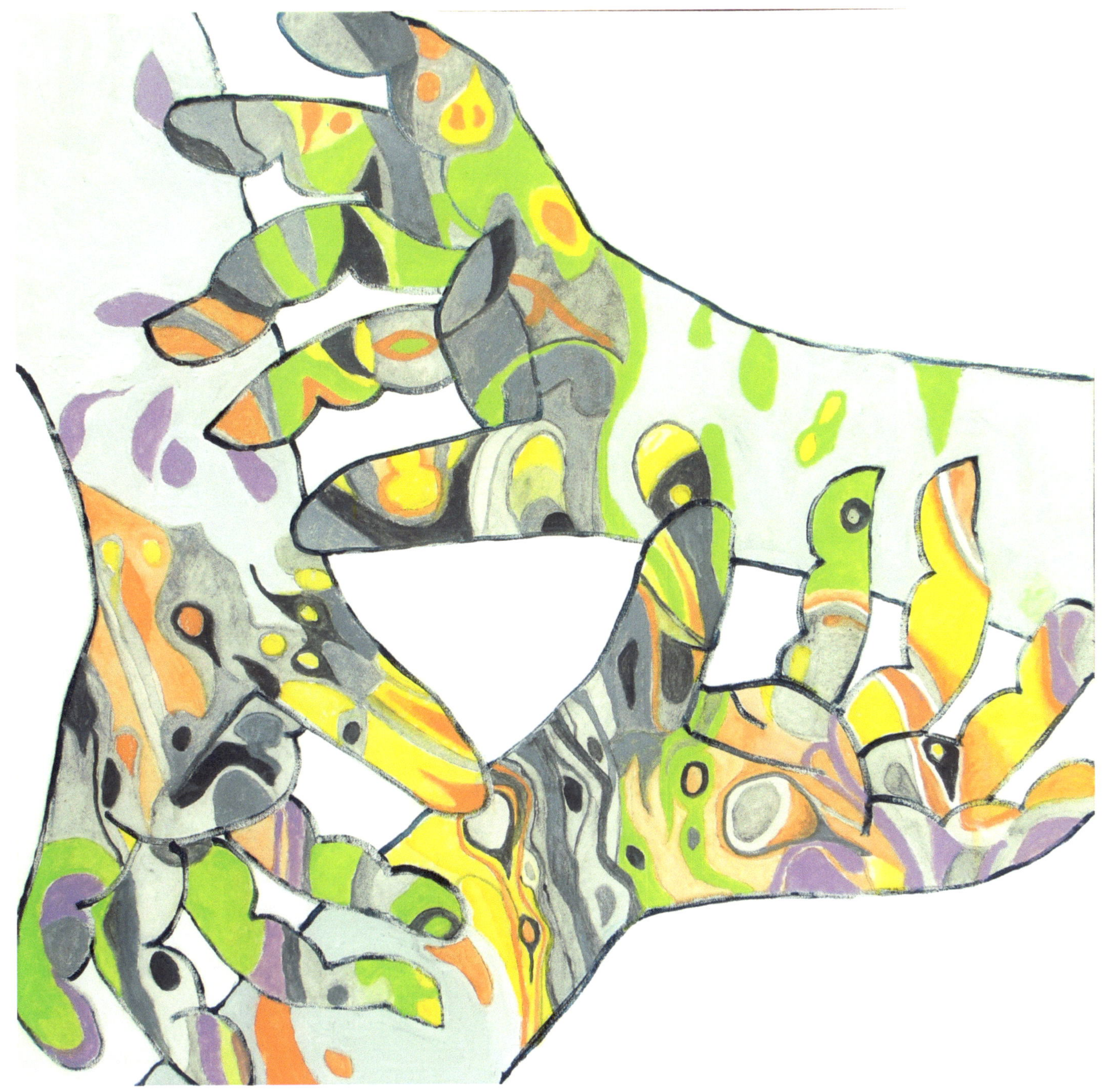

46 Years Old, Sculpting Hands

I need to use my creative expression in order to balance my life. I have been making sculptures since my separation with my husband. My Nature series was chosen as one of the best in a gallery opening. The fine proportion is formed like the natural elements, wind, and water. It is an immediate expression of nature. In this painting, my hands are moving fast to form an immediate expression of the objects. The soap bubble fractal represents the underlying fractal nature of the natural world.

Acrylic on Canvas 36x36 inch

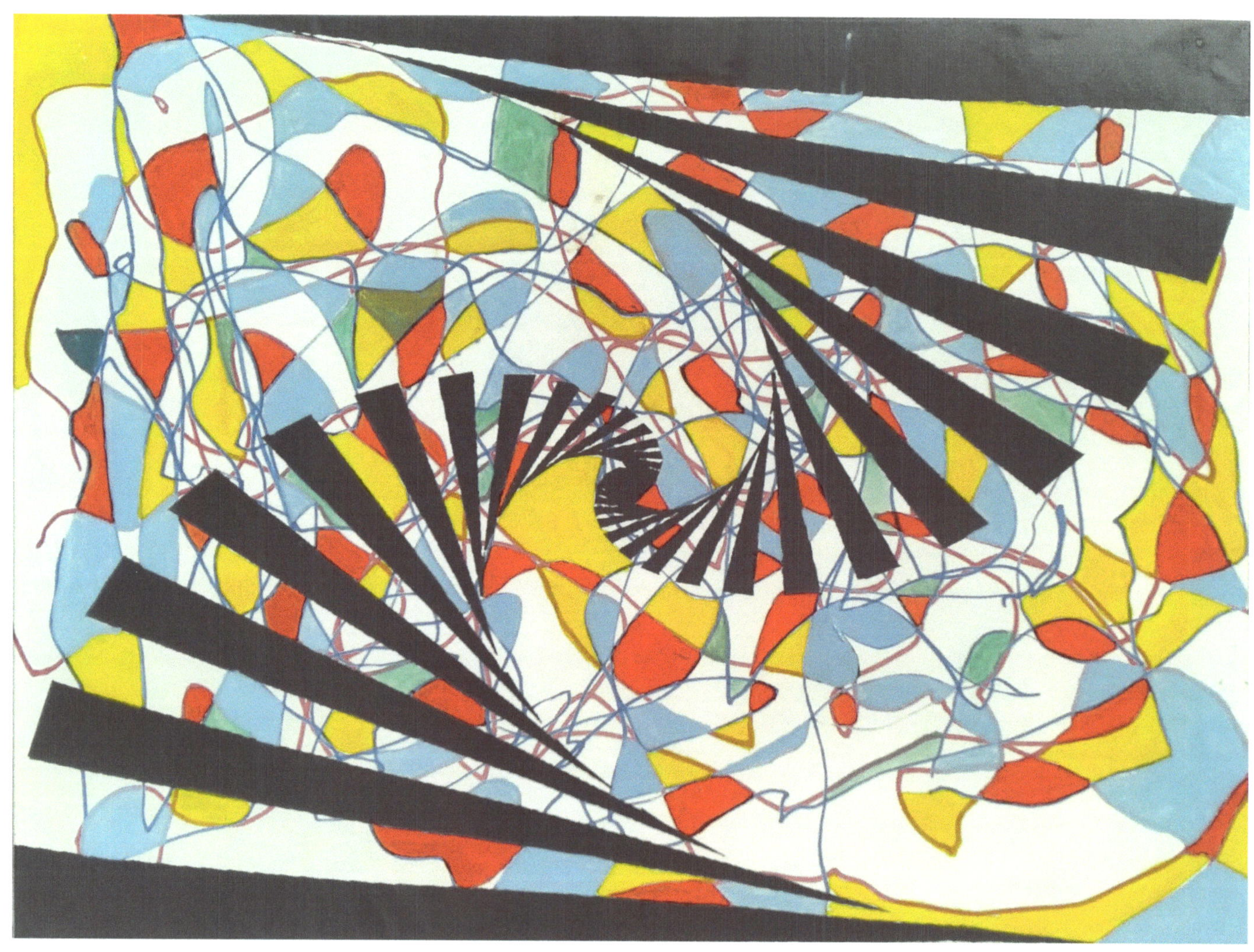

47 Years Old, Balancing Life

My Life can be more balanced now. The labor of making a big sculpture is too intense. So I decided to change to painting. Now I can also incorporate color to represent my emotions. I have a job doing no such creative work but my life becomes more regular with less stress. I still miss the design aspect of my work. Balancing life is always delicate, My son Adam is growing beautifully and I get a lot of pleasure seeing him thrive. In this painting, the chaotic and fractal-like variations of my life are being replaced by a uniform spiral leading me to a new more stable life in the future.

Acrylic on Canvas 40x30 inch

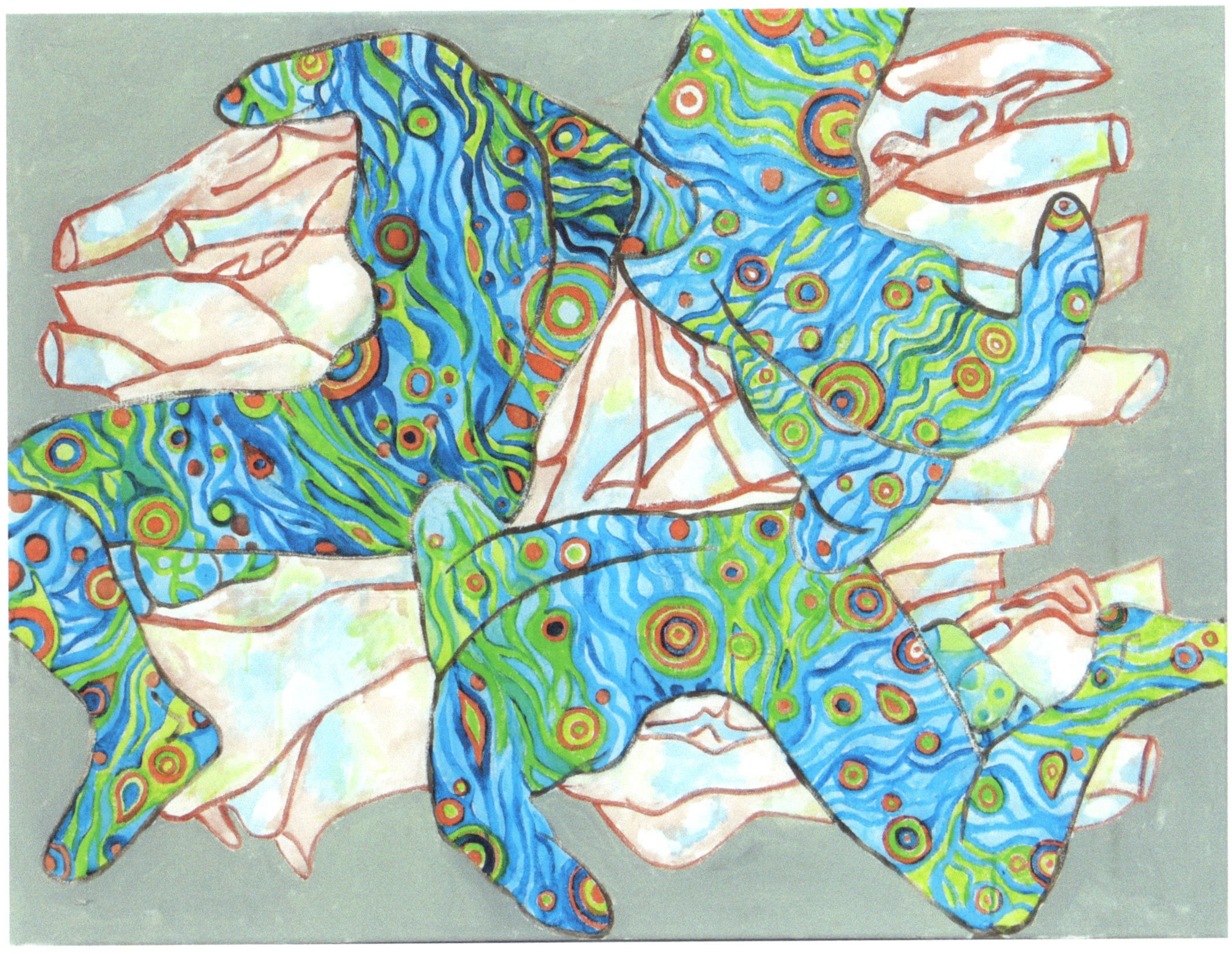

48 Years Old, Boring Job

I had worked at a job that was the most boring. I just needed a job to pay the bills, a regular work job. I had a hard time staying awake doing the work. Sometimes there was space planning but most of the time the work was not creative at all. This painting looks more interesting than my job. I got a lot of pleasure doing design work at other jobs so I am using this painting as a distraction from the boring work.

Acrylic on Canvas 40x30 inch

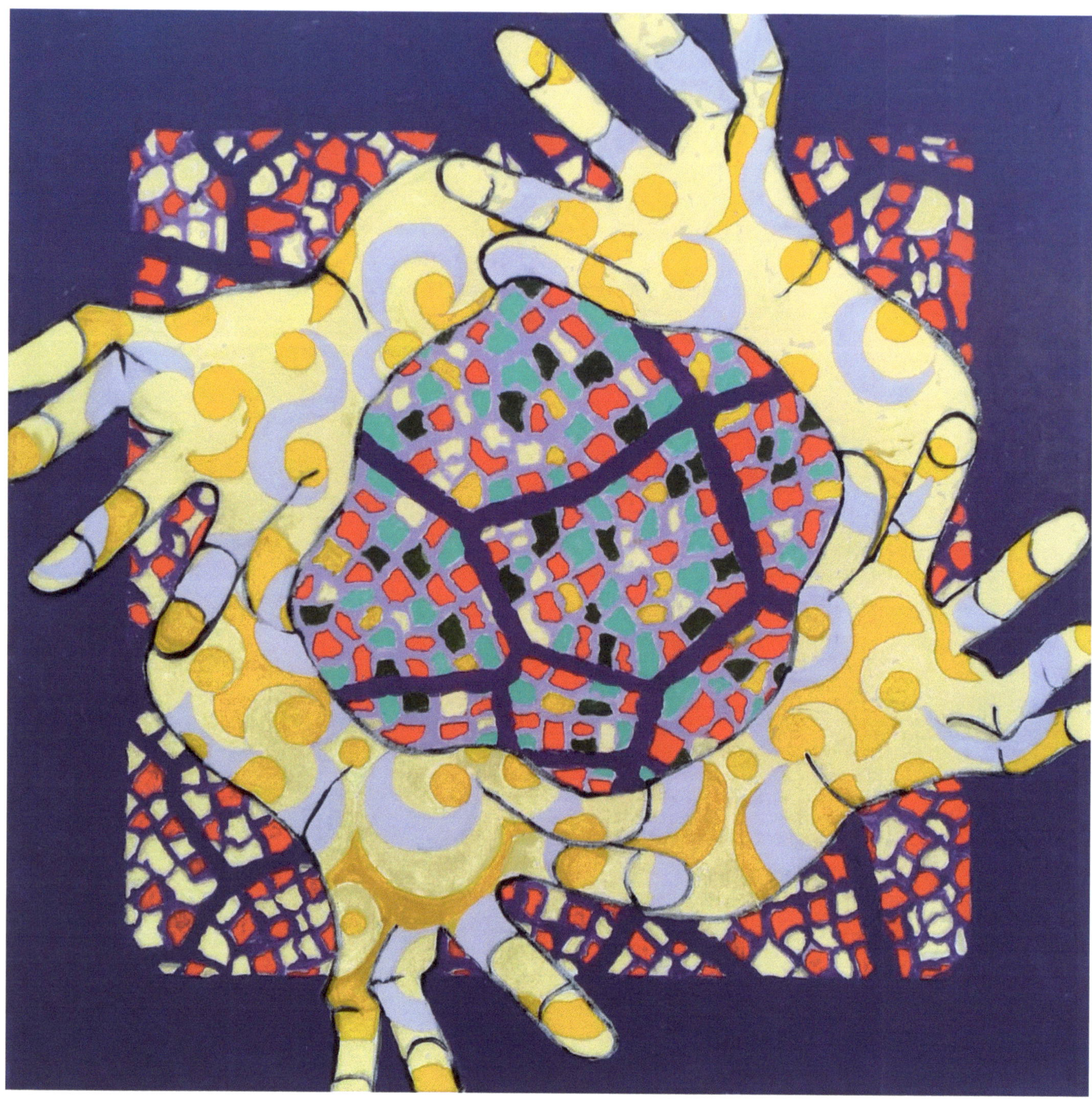

49 Years Old, Traveling

I love traveling, I enjoy being away and thinking about my life. Guatemala is perfect to visit since all the cultures and the Mayan temples are so different. How the people live in different ways and have different beliefs? I have not been focused on my life in New York and its surroundings. I am definitely getting to have a more organized life. In this painting, the hands are traveling the world touching the varied cultures. Touching the culture and understanding the culture is very important.

Acrylic on Canvas 36x36 inch

Chapter 5 – Recovery

My art was giving me a purpose in life. I was confident in my art but was not sure that the confidence was real or a side affect of medication. Winning prestigious awards for my painting work cemented the confidence in reality and I was able to move on with my creativity.

I met Peter at dancing lessons and he established a close and bonding relationship with my son Adam. The visitations I was allowed with Adam developed into adventures and trips out hiking in the mountains. I bonded closely with Adam and was able to take trips with just mother and son to places like Paris where I remembered my young years and could share those memories with him.

I remarried with Peter and we started a life together. He supported my art work and I was contented and moving forward with life again.

The paintings in this chapter cover years 50 through 55, recovery and developing a new life.

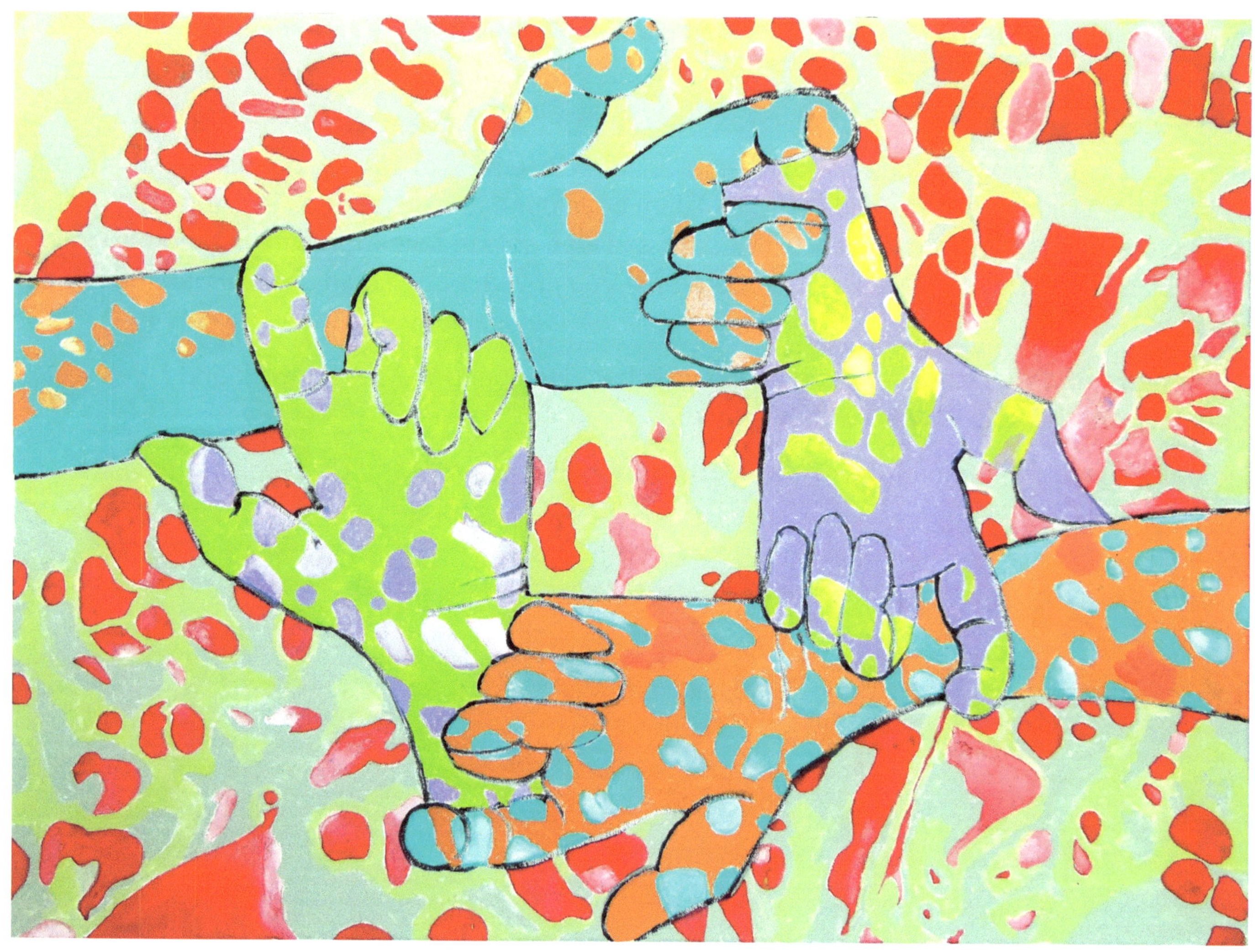

50 Years Old, One Spring Day with Peter

The spring is so beautiful showing the rebirth everywhere. Fractal shapes are exquisite structures produced by nature, hiding in plain sight all around us. Peter and my feelings are growing and we are putting down roots that will be ready to flower. We are so happy to see spring-like flowers blooming in our lives. The tafoni in this painting give mathematical harmony in the background. The tafoni are converted to red petals linking tafoni rock to spring flowers to human hands. Tafoni are holes in rocks, the holes vary in size and depth. I am inspired by the patterns created by tafoni.

Acrylic on Canvas 40x30 inch

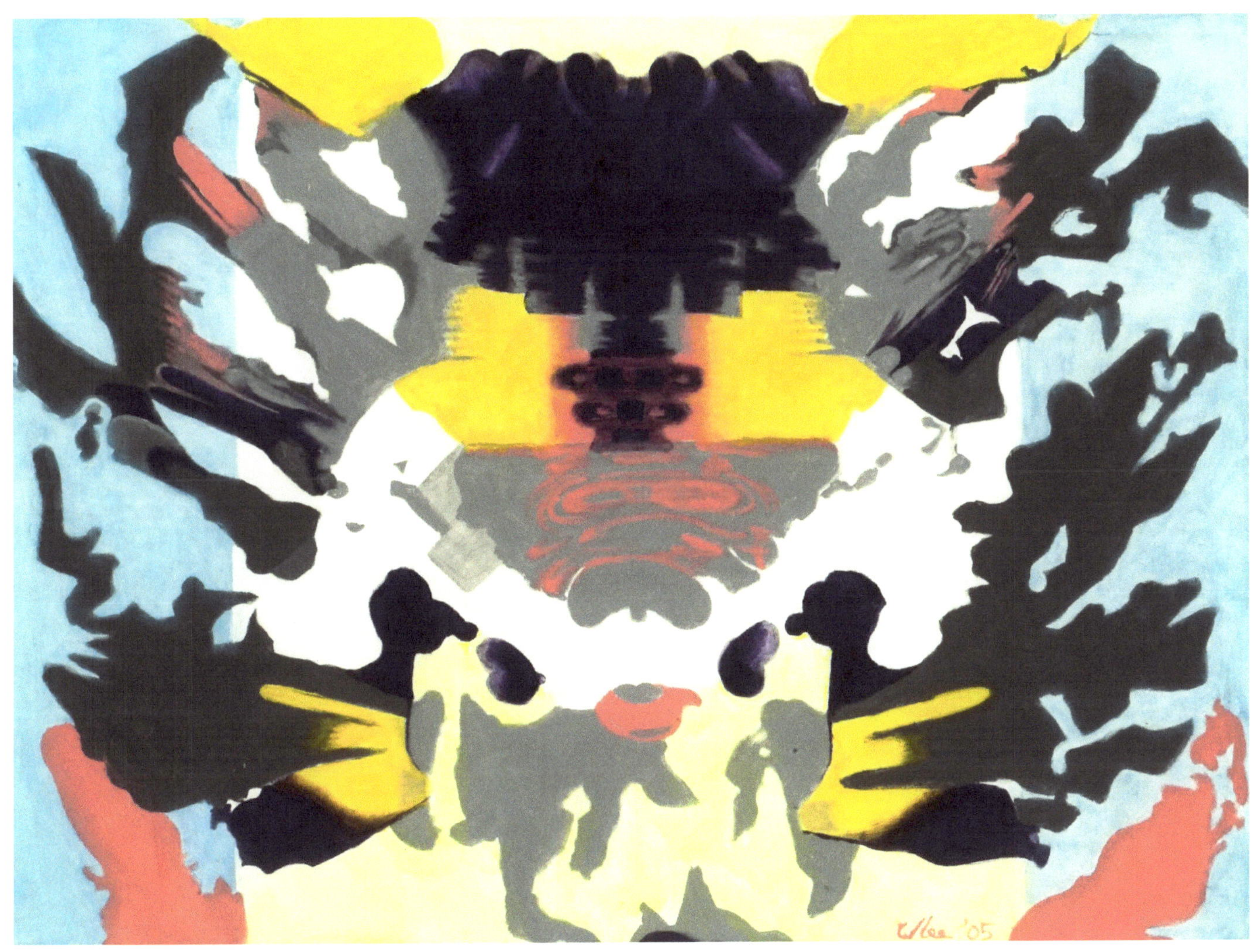

51 Years Old, I Won an Award For My Painting

I won the grand competition at the Art Student League in New York City and received a $6,000 award. I was amazed at the fact that my paintings were chosen this year. I was anticipating winning the competition next year. I have had all sorts of life troubles but there is one thing that has been consistent, that was my love of painting. I have painted all the time no matter what the situation is in my life. I felt that I was at the top of my game and getting an award has given me the confidence to pursue what I like. My goal is set and I am running towards my goal and destiny. I like painting more than design because I can sign the painting with my own name.

Acrylic on Canvas 40x30 inch

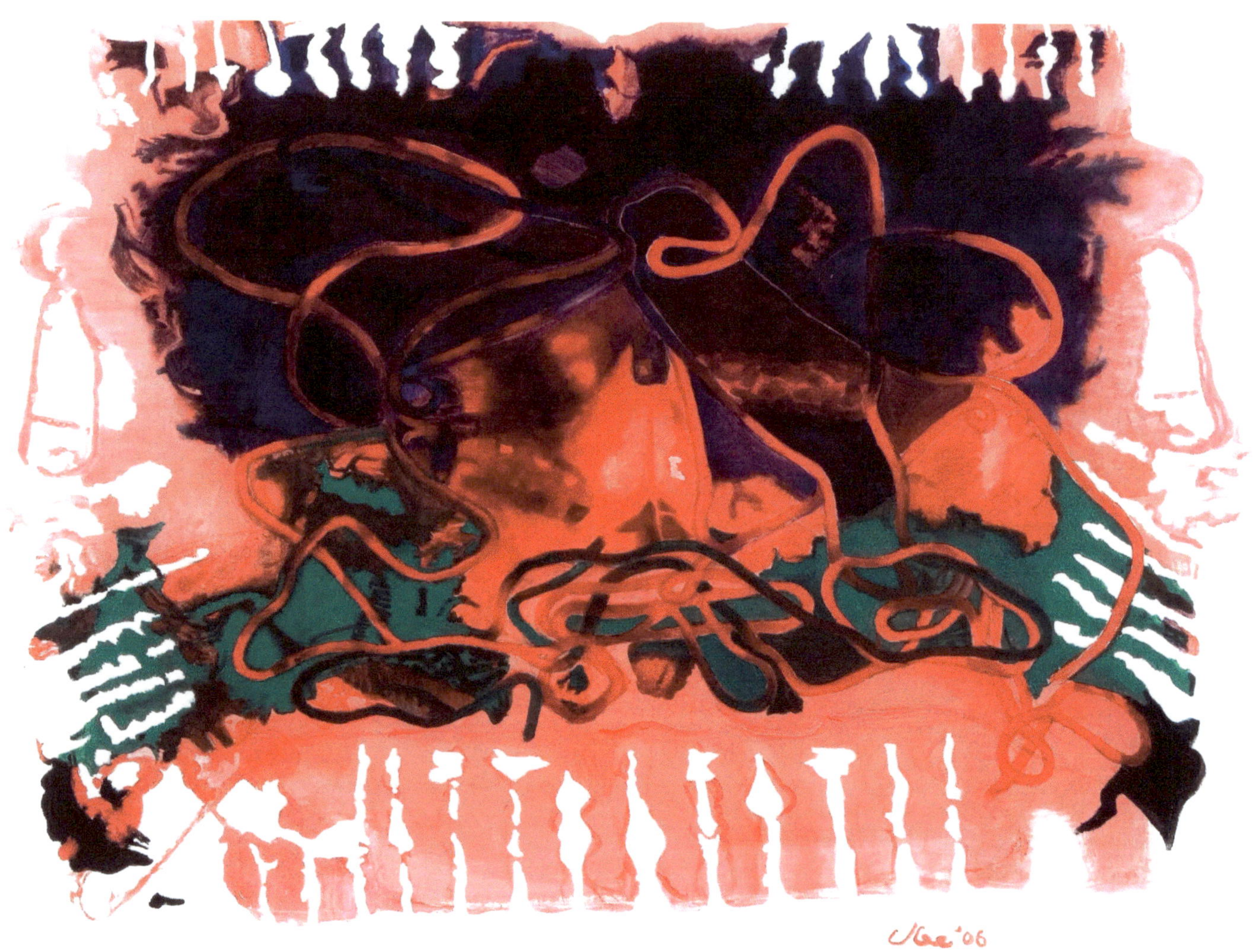

52 Years Old, Another Competition

In my 52nd year I won another art award. I was anticipating another award. I have been very serious about my paintings since the previous award last year and have received positive feedback. Now I finally know what direction I should take in my life. My confidence in my paintings has grown more and more. When I studied at Parsons School of Design I always liked painting as well as my major in Interior Architecture. I finally feel that I have returned to painting and feel very comfortable with that.

Acrylic on Canvas 40x30 inch

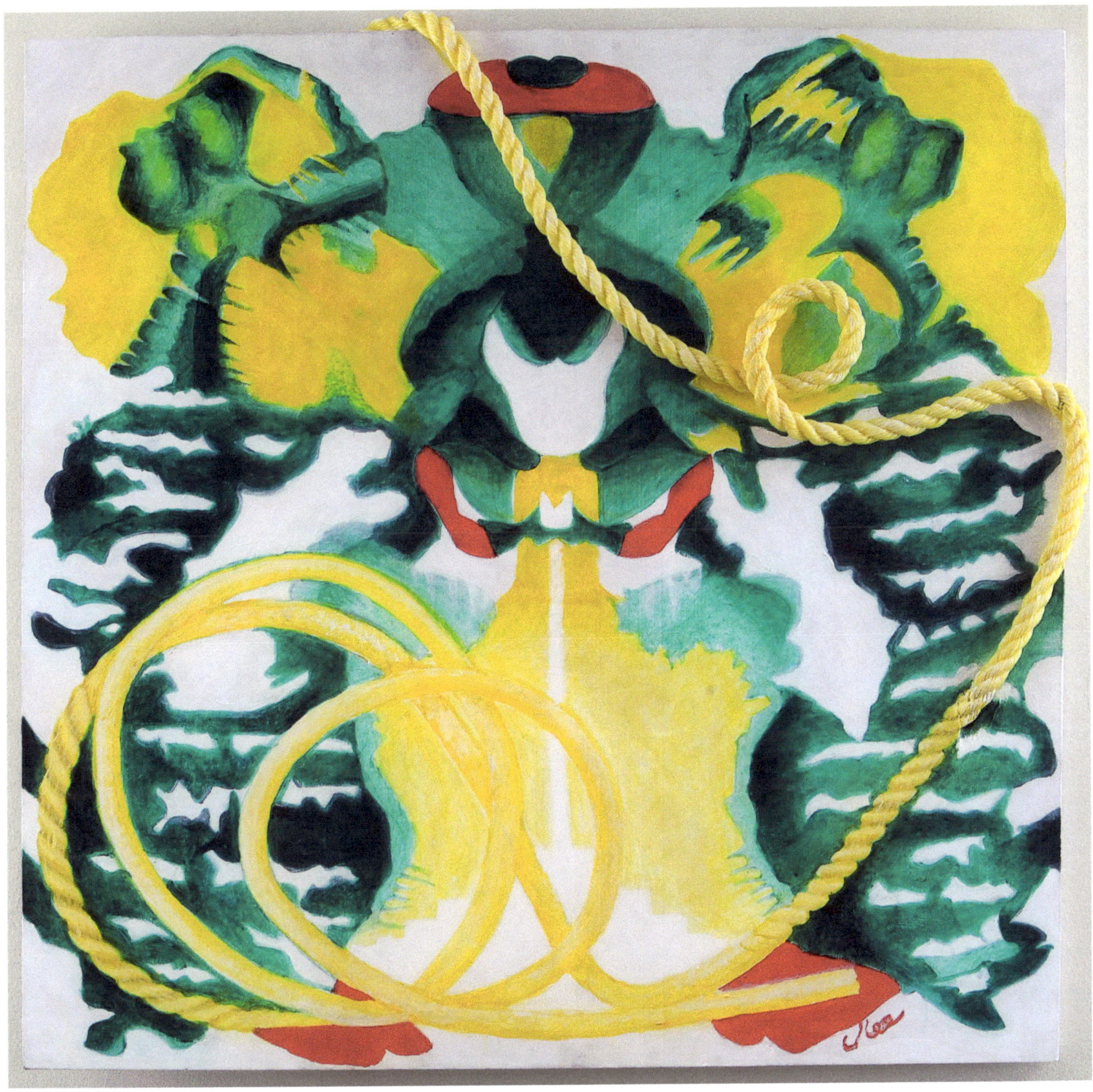

53 Years Old, Visitation

The time I spend together with my son "Adam" is so precious. I enjoy every minute of it. He is such a good conversationalist even at his young age. We are bound together all the time. He is very sensitive and is very much like my own personality. He is thinking of being a musician but he is not sure yet. The painting shows the excitement of being together and sharing music. We are bound together!

Acrylic on Canvas 36x36 inch

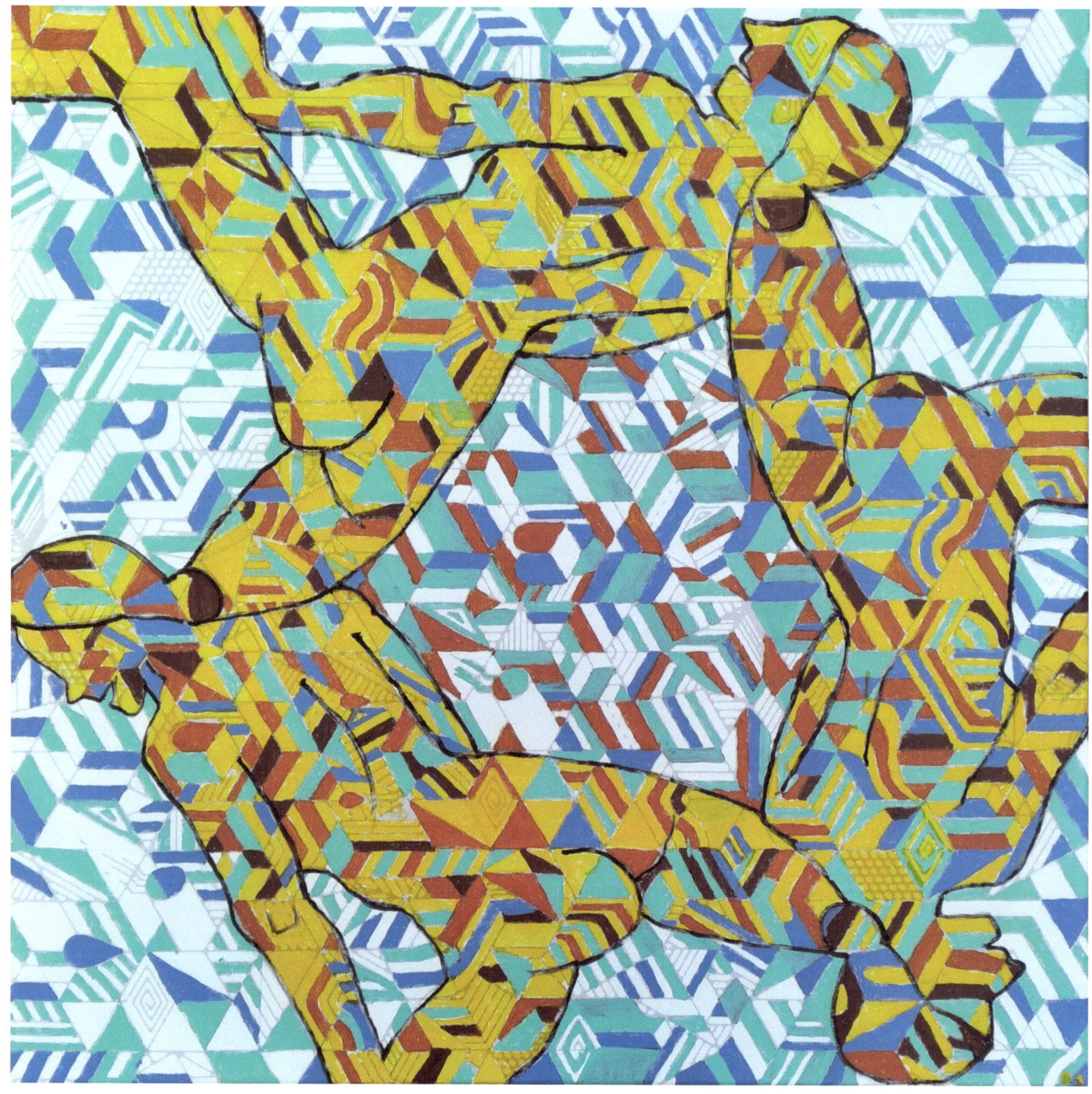

54 Years Old, Geometry Woman

I finally feel my life is coming back together I am very balanced in my life as a single person. I am supporting myself working as a designer and my son, Adam, is growing beautifully. I took Adam to Paris on his birthday. I took him to the Eiffel Tower for a birthday dinner. He was so excited to have a birthday dinner at the Eiffel Tower. I won two art competitions and Peter and I decided to get married next year. It is good that I have got a balanced geometry to my life and everything is moving in a good direction after my mighty difficult times.

Acrylic on Canvas 36x36 inch

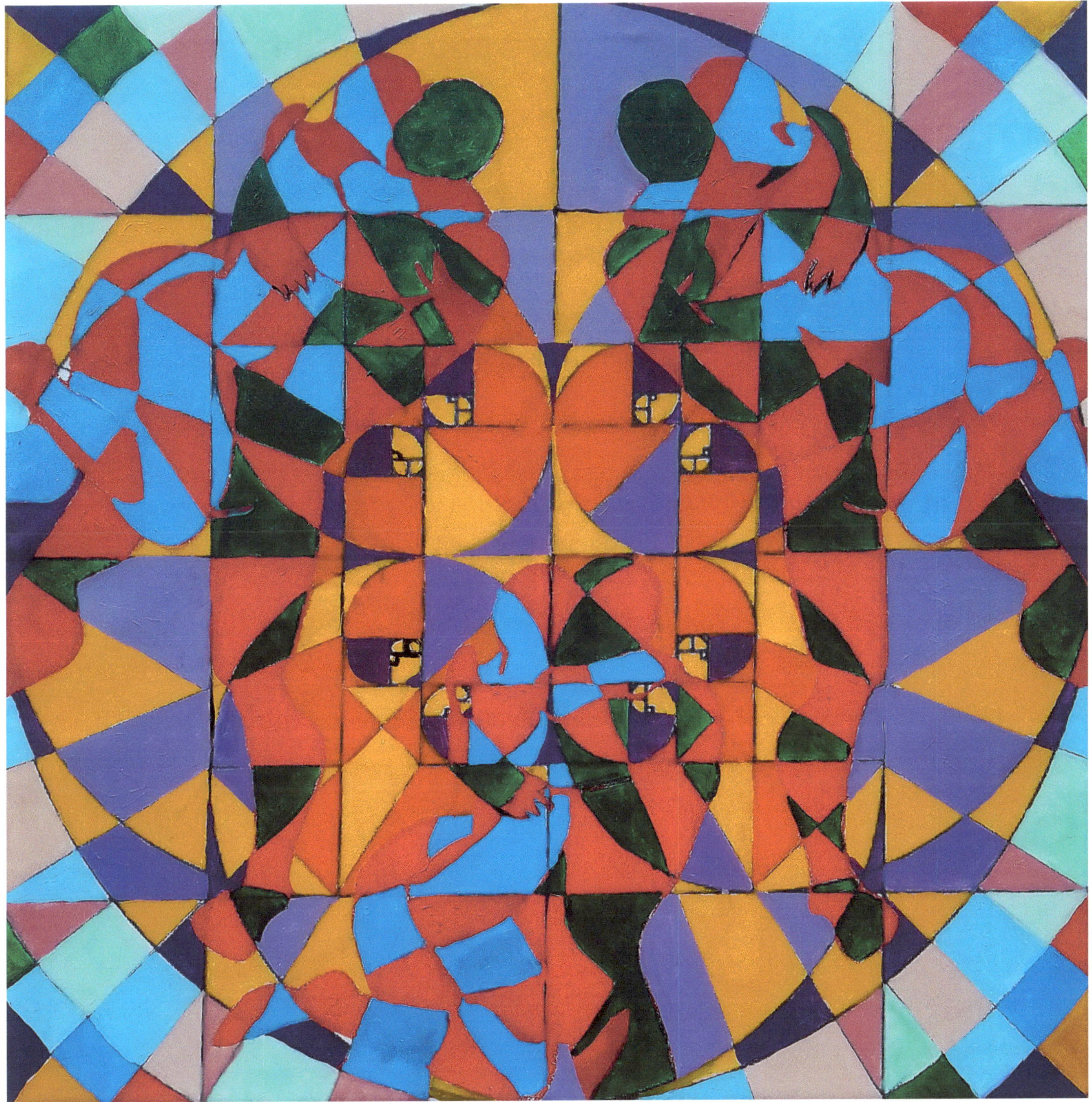

55 Years Old, Remarry

It has been 16 years since I became single again. I believe in marriage so I always thought I would find a special person in 2 or 3 years since I know the kind of person I am looking for. I met Peter almost right away but I could not see him as my partner. We spent 15 years together as friends without thinking of marriage. Finally, when he proposed to me I was with another person. But I knew that Peter is the one I should spend the rest of my life with. This painting represents traditional Korean wedding clothes. We got married in a traditional wedding ceremony in an outdoor museum in Seoul.

Acrylic on Canvas 39x39 inch

Chapter 6 – Adventure and experiences

My life is back together, I was thriving again, I had dreams and hope for the future.

After Peter retired we set off in our sail boat and sailed from New York City down to the Caribbean. We spent three years exploring the coast of the USA and the Caribbean Islands and had many adventures and met many interesting people.

I got immense inspiration for my art and developed new ideas and concepts.

Adam, my son, married a wonderful woman and his life was developing marvelously. He was training to be a medical doctor and enjoyed every minute of his life. That was a great inspiration for me.

We lived through Hurricanes Irma and Maria in the Caribbean while living on our boat. We purchased some distressed properties in Puerto Rico that were damaged by the Hurricanes. We renovated them and I was able to utilize my Interior Design skills to create unique and interesting homes.

The dreams were back, I had a future, and I am enjoying life.

I have recovered.

The paintings in this chapter cover years 56 through 68, adventure and recovery.

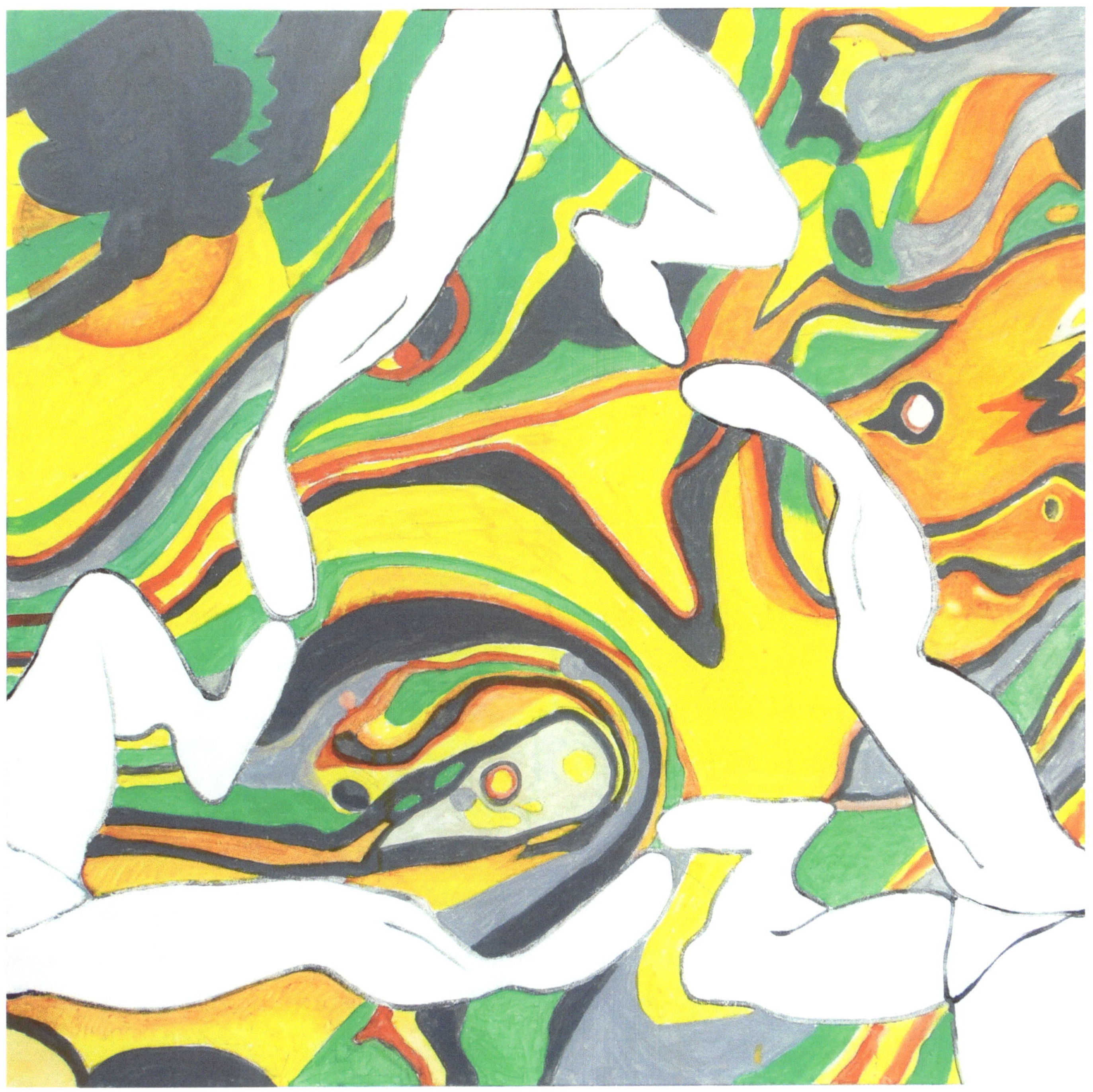

56 Years Old, Dancing in the Moonlight

It was in Mexico with a beautiful full moon shining over the ocean. We were walking along the beach and the music lead us into a beach restaurant. The owner brought the table down the beach and into one-foot deep water. We were intrigued by everything and ordered what they suggested. We stood up from the table and started dancing in the moonlight. The beautiful moon shines on us with romantic moonbeams, the fish dish served to us was delicious. This is another now in the present time that connects to the forever moment of life.

Acrylic on Canvas 36x36 inch

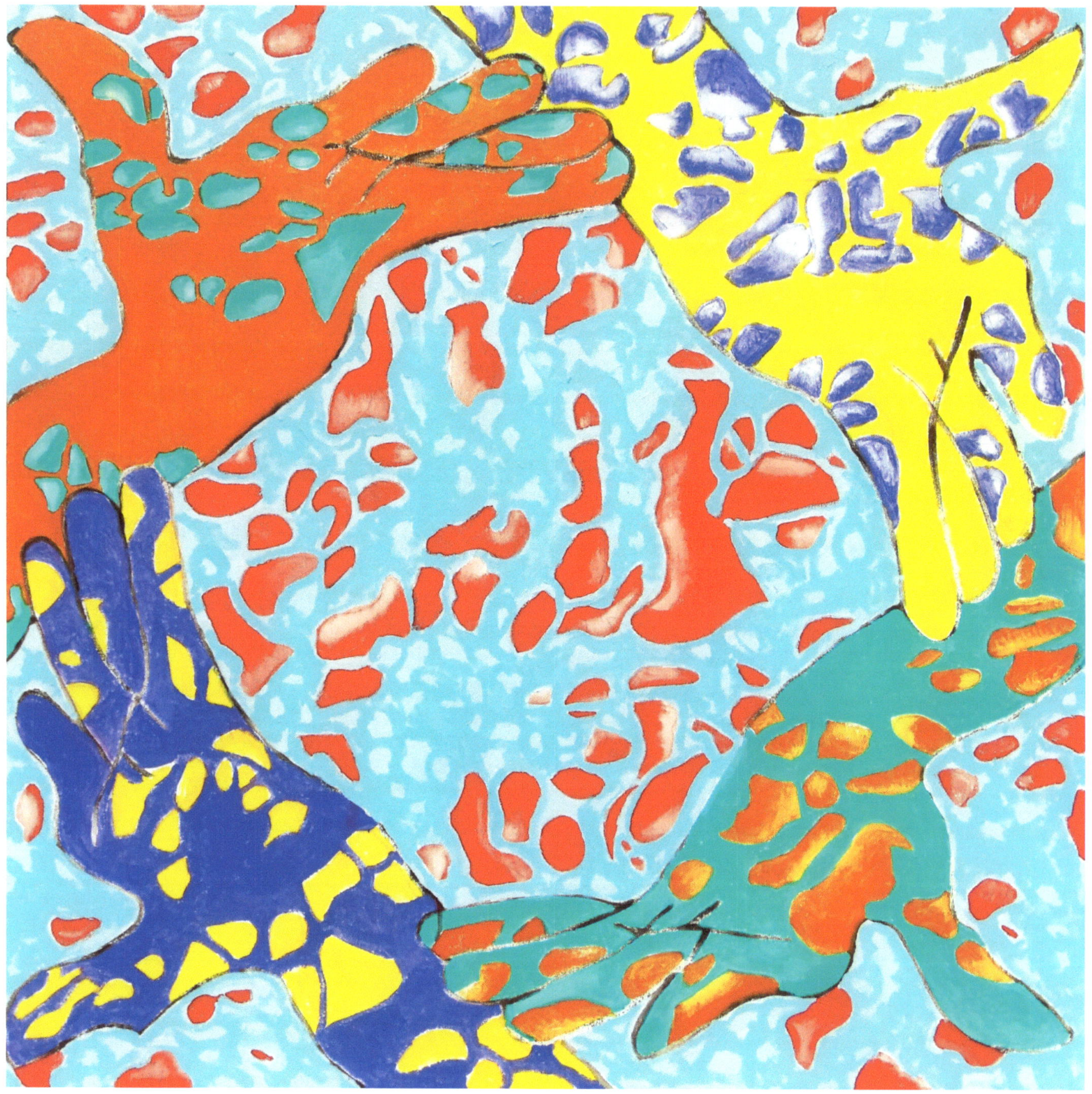

57 Years Old, One Summer Day With Peter

One summer day Peter and I had a moment to have a beautiful bonded feeling. Every part of the world was beautiful and rosy. It is a very delicate moment and we are aware of everything around us. We have been together for a long time. Finally, we realized that we are happier together. Our hands are basking in bright summer sun rays. Our emotions are flying around like confetti, our hands are chasing each other in a dance. This summer day will connect to the forever moment in our lives.

Acrylic on Canvas 36x36 inch

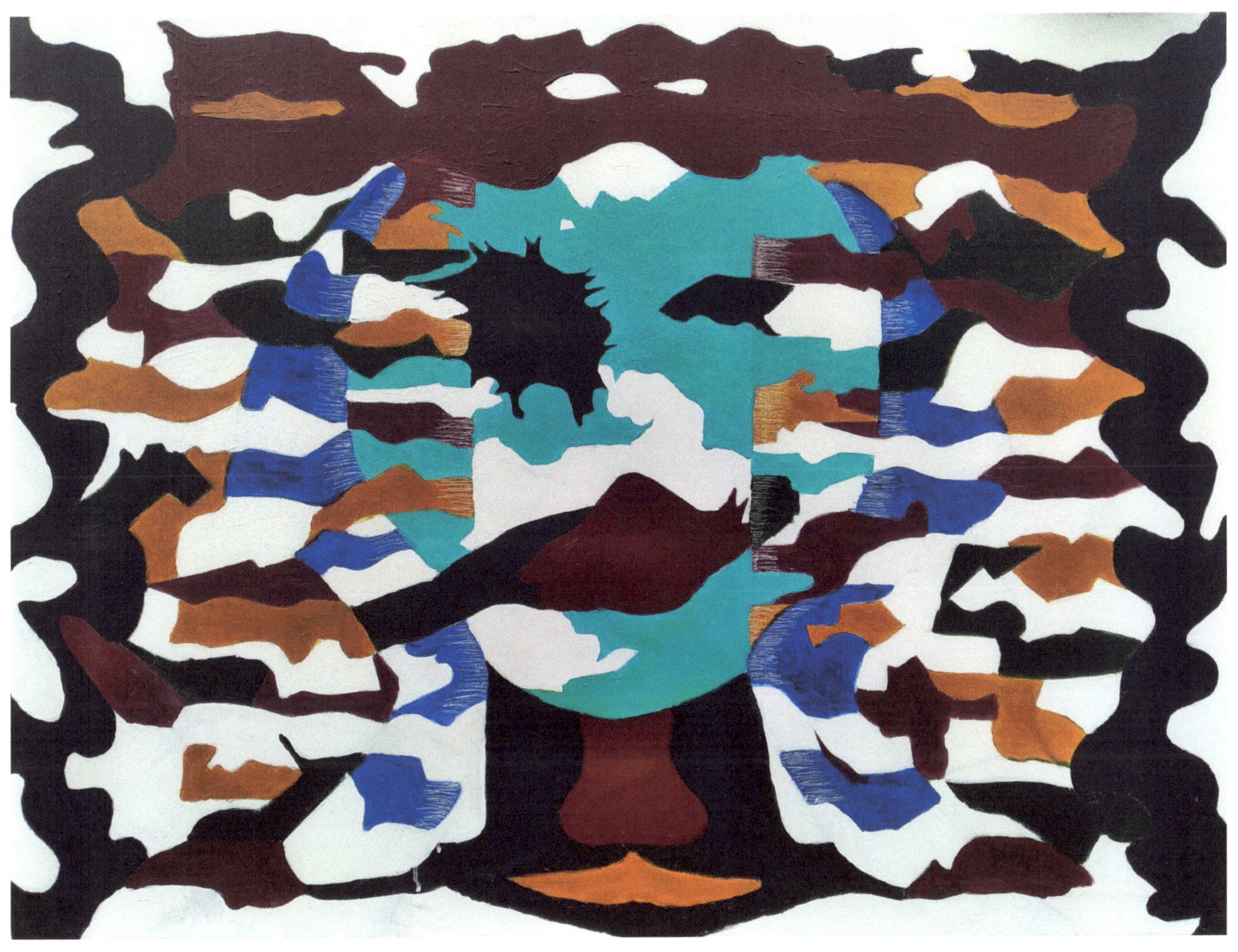

58 Years Old, Teacher and Me

Life is sometimes complicated and goes in different directions. In the end, everything settles down and the experience is remaining. Clearly, all the peaceful thoughts are layered on life. No regrets and no sadness laid layer by layer in the rich tapestry of life. The happy and yet sad face is smiling and crying. It is however in peace and gets over everything that happens in life.

Acrylic on Canvas 48x36 inch

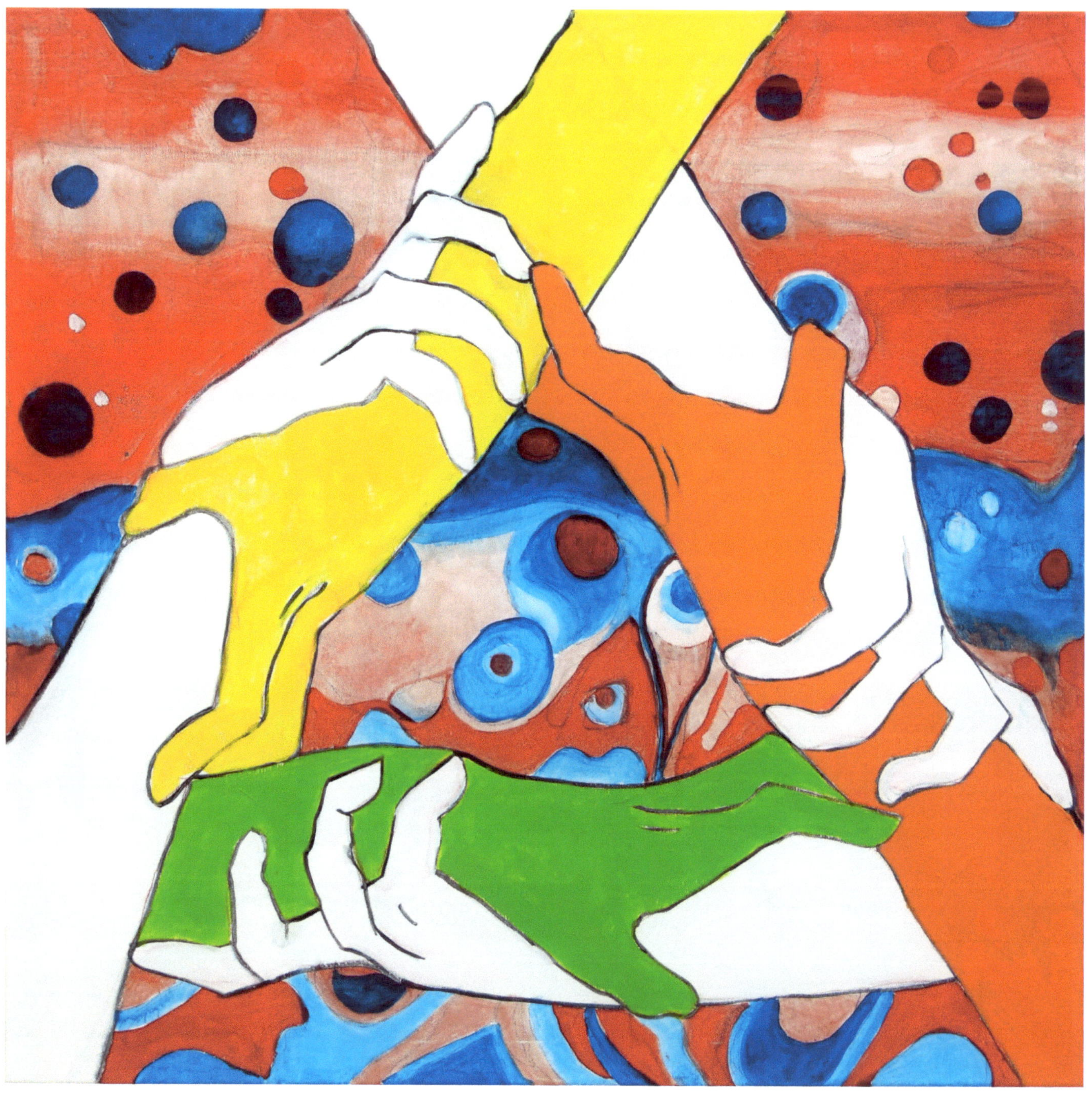

59 Years Old, Grabbing Hands

We, my sisters and I, have similar backgrounds but developed three very different personalities. Our different early life experiences developed us differently but we are always supportive of each other. All our different dreams are shared with each other and thus we influenced and helped each other. We were grabbing hands as we grew up together. Helping each other experience the first piece of life. Especially when we needed the support of each other. On the eve of my sixtieth birthday, I have fond memories of these younger days.

Acrylic on Canvas 36x36 inch

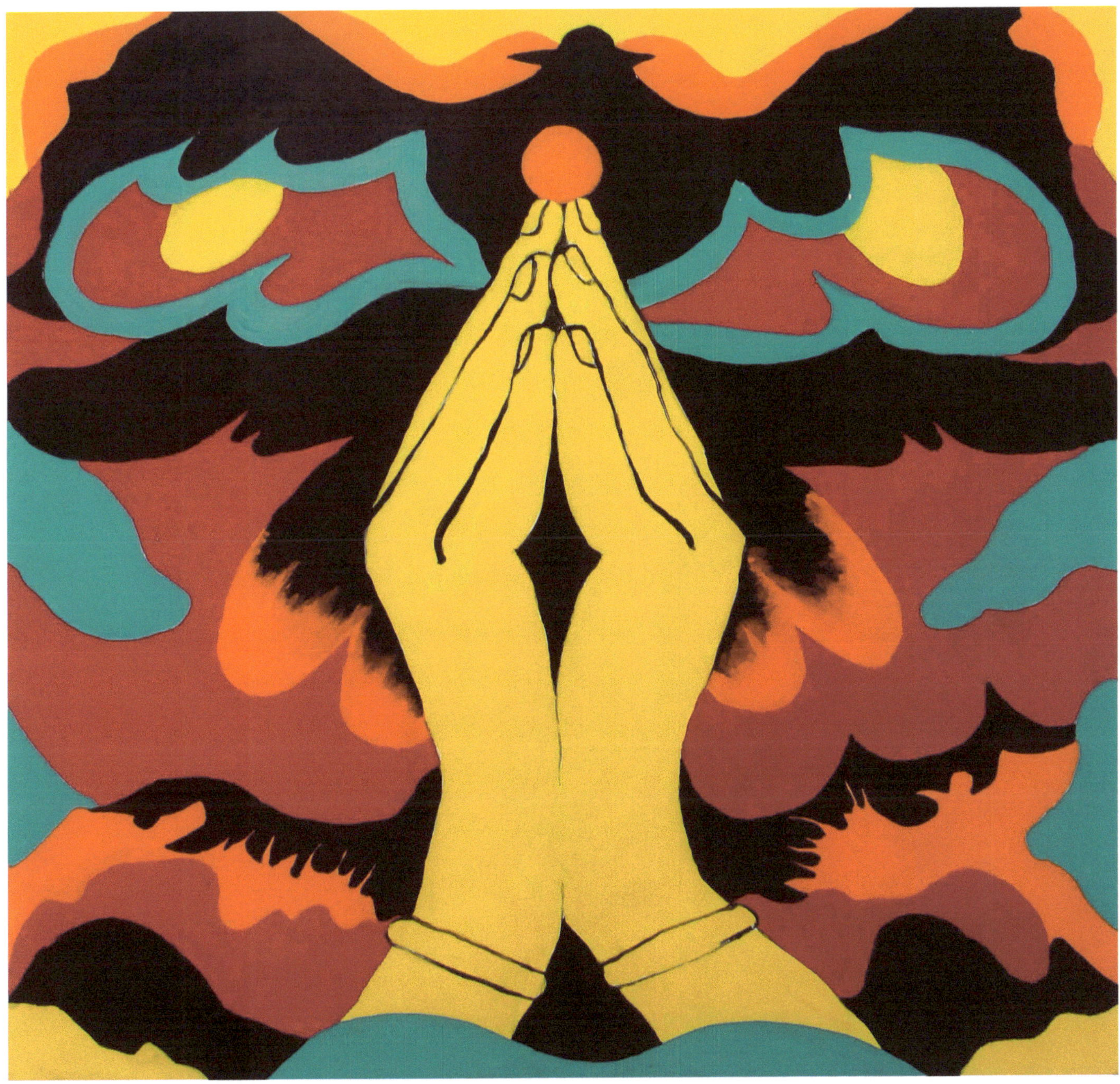

60 Years Old, India!

I made a trip to India in my 60th year. India has a fascinating culture and people. It is so different from any other place in the world. The interaction with animals can be so deep and penetrates directly into social life. The eyes of the people have the eyes of a fierce wild animal and at the same time a controlling calmness. Greetings between people introduces any and all human emotions derived from this multicolored culture.

Acrylic on Canvas 36x36 inch

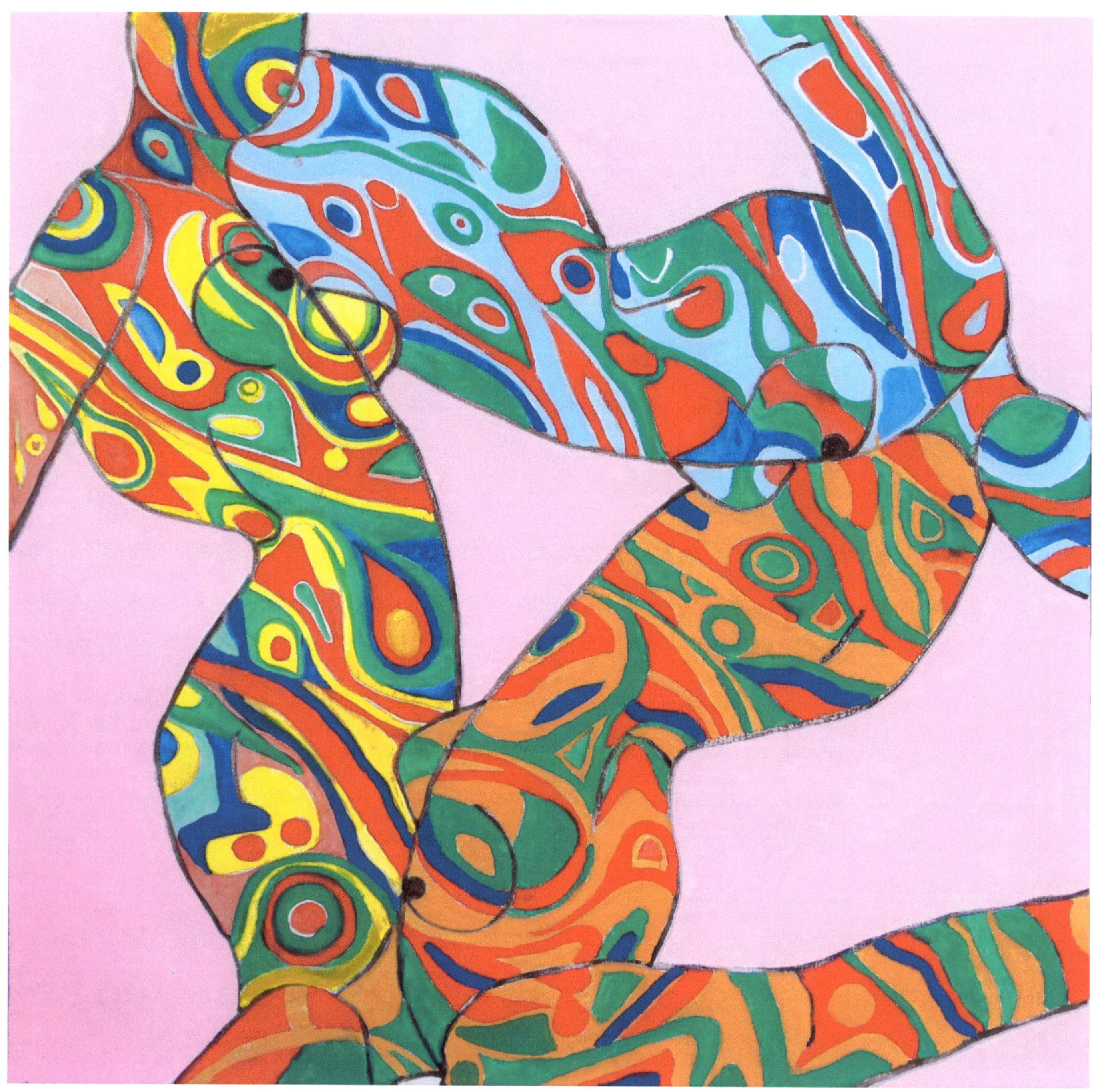

61 Years Old, Three Women

Three women covered in fractal bubbles create an interesting juxtaposition. The way they are arranged creates a warm and friendly relationship. The colors in the bubbles are created by light interference representing our interactions in life. This is the ideal position for us, the three sisters. The shapes of the bubbles are similar but the colors of the bodies are completely different just like our personalities.

Acrylic on Canvas 36x36 inch

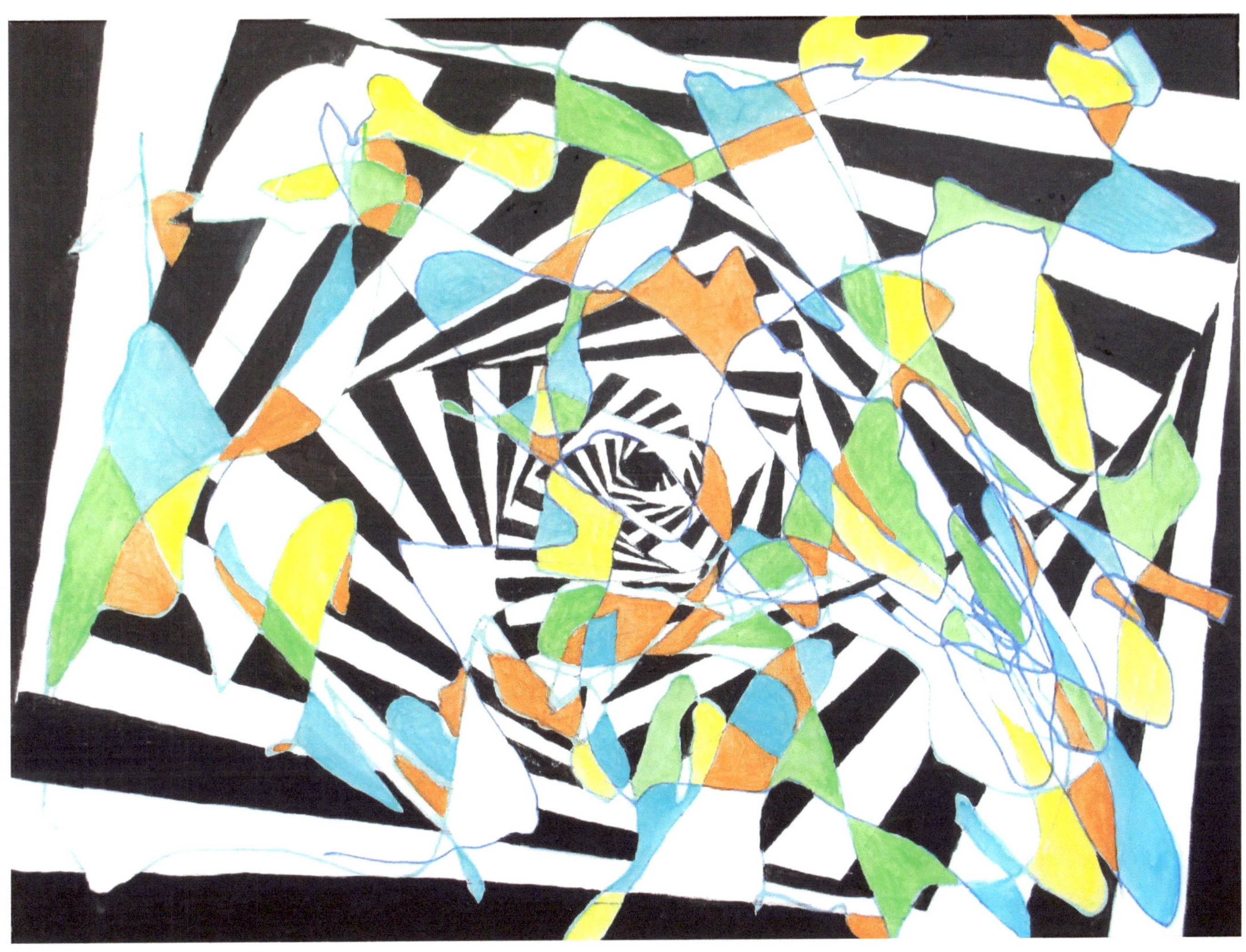

62 Years Old, Sailing

Sailing, most of the time, is smooth and gliding between the waves. The boat is gently uplifted and advances quietly towards a distant destination powered by the wind. We cruised our sailboat "Notre Voyage" for 3 years from New York City to the Caribbean. It is hard to make a straight line when sailing so I did just the opposite and allowed the moving boat to guide my hand. All the lines are gentle movements with the fractal spiral representing the wind and waves that create the motion. The wave lines inspired

Acrylic on Canvas 40x30 inch

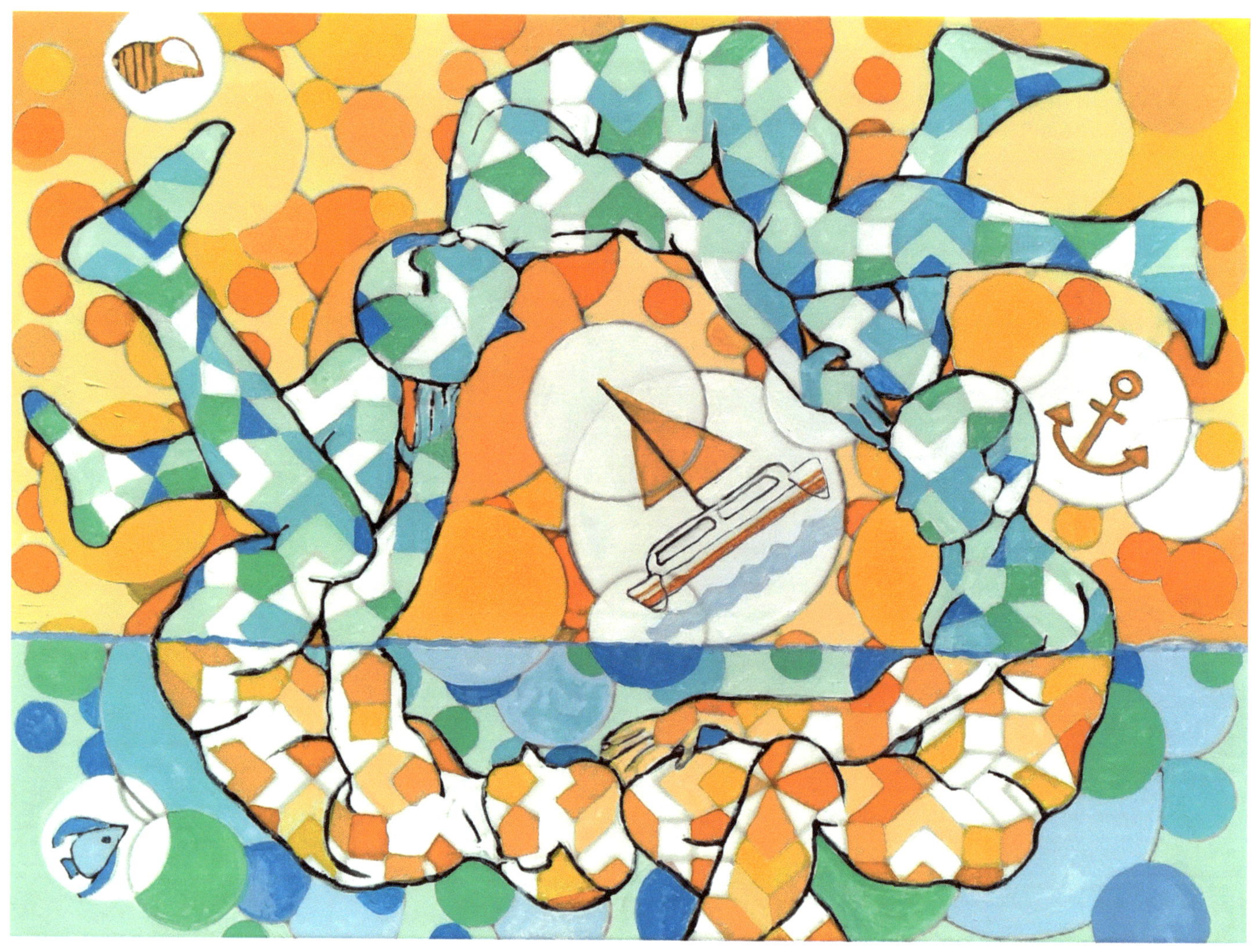

63 Years Old, Peter Sailing

We sailed our sailboat “Notre Voyage” from New York to the Caribbean. We sailed around the Caribbean for 3 years. The overnight sailing is the toughest thing for us, we exchanged lookout every 4 hours so sleep is a luxury. That makes arriving at an isolated Caribbean beach with still waters and palm trees especially wonderful. The Caribbean has warm bright sunshine. Peter is busy in the water and out of the water. He is always prepared for the sailing chores. Cleaning the fish, and conch, and checking the anchor, he is always a sailing expert.

Acrylic on Canvas 40x30 inch

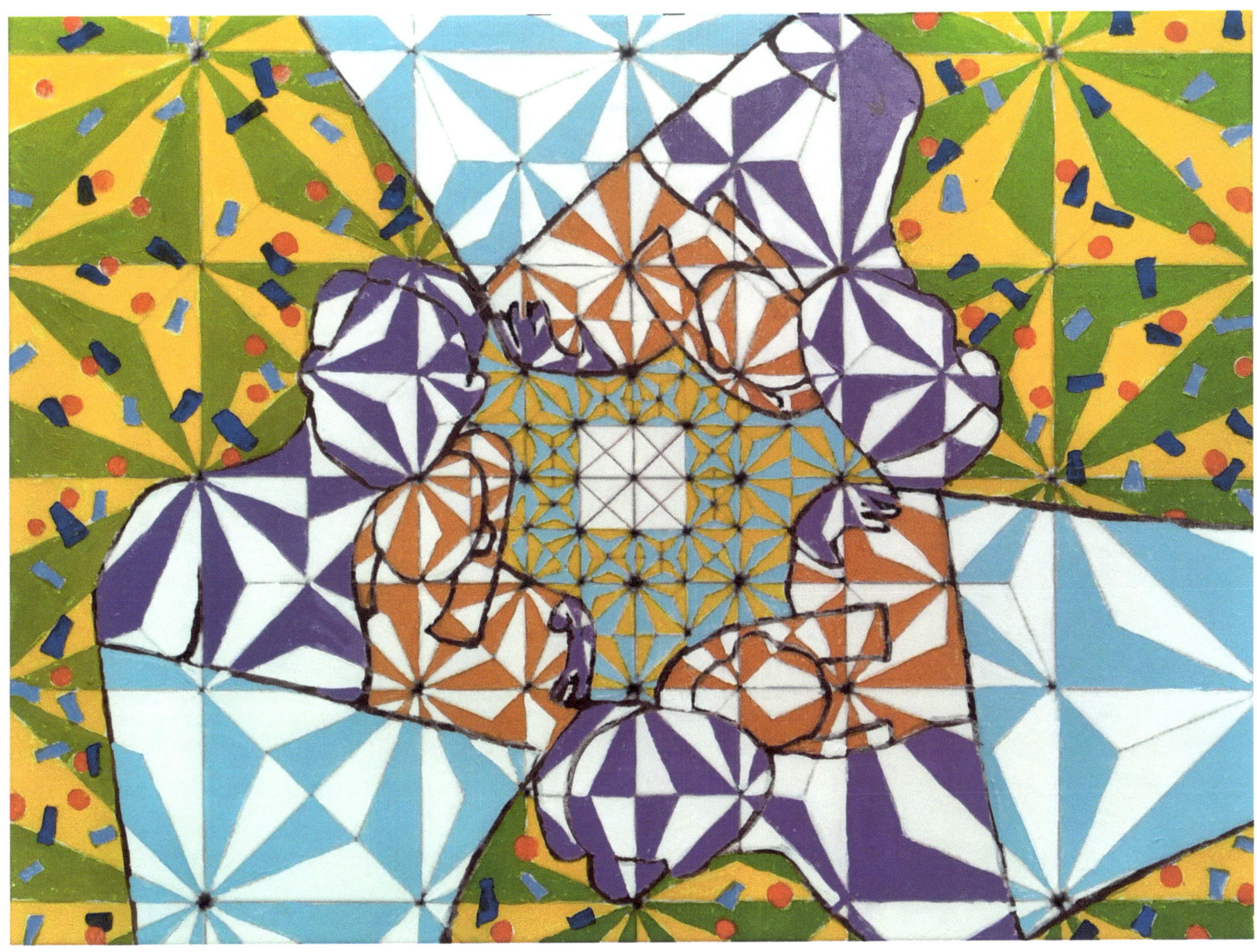

64 Years Old, My Son's Wedding

It was a gorgeous day in New Hampshire during the summer of 2017. The wedding day of my son! I am inspired to do many paintings, sparkling lake, happy people, family together. I settled on one image that conjures up the sparkle of that day. I wish them all my love and hopes for a long and happy marriage. There is Adam and Jenny, a light blue tie worn by Adam, and a white wedding dress worn by Jenny. Jennie's color comes from the bouquet she holds with a white background. The shape holding them is a granite sarcophagus to celebrate eternal love and life.

Acrylic on Canvas 40x30 inch

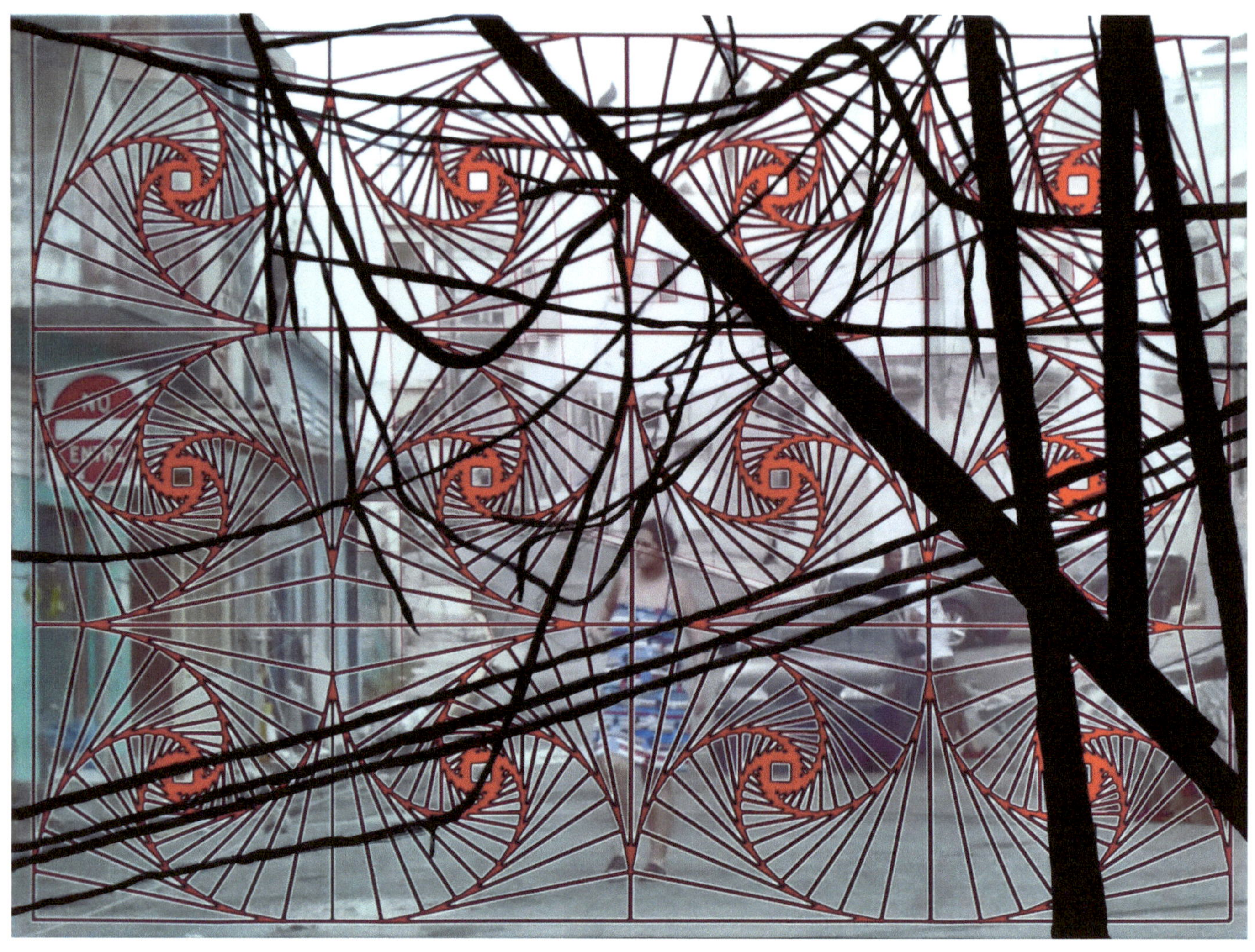

65 Years Old, Hurricane Maria

Hurricane Maria in Puerto Rico was so powerful that everything was upside down after the hurricane. The experience of the feeling of a Hurricane shaking the big stone building was so terrifying. The Category 5 Hurricane tore off most of the leaves from the tree trunks. The mountains and hills were completely brown in color due to the leaves being all torn apart. It looked like winter but there is no winter in Puerto Rico. For a while, the Puertorican streets are all like this painting. The electricity was not restored completely for 8 months. The painting shows how normal life faded away replaced by memories of the tormenta and broken power lines.

Acrylic on Canvas 40x30 inch

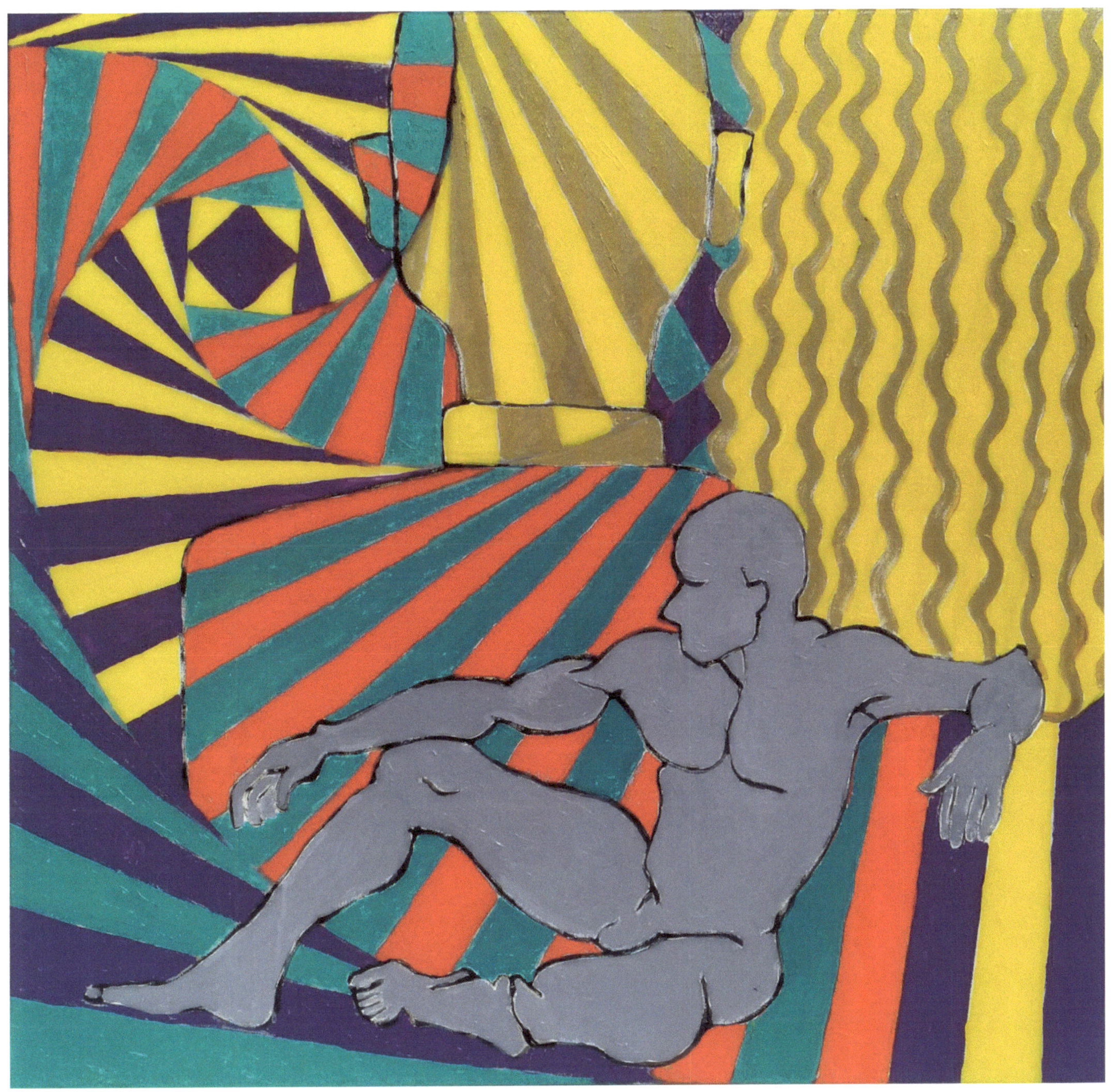

66 Years Old, Friends in Villa

We often enjoyed long dinners with these friends in the garden. We talked about relationships on a philosophical level with a lot of laughs. During the Pandemic, it is hard to socialize but we were having a marvelous time together with ice-cold sangria sips that they had prepared. Their backs are so beautiful and graceful. She has fantastically curly blond hair that is outstandingly beautiful. He is sitting on the fractal curve and seems to enjoy his thoughts. The thoughts are also fractal just like a stock market graphic.

Acrylic on Canvas 36x36 inch

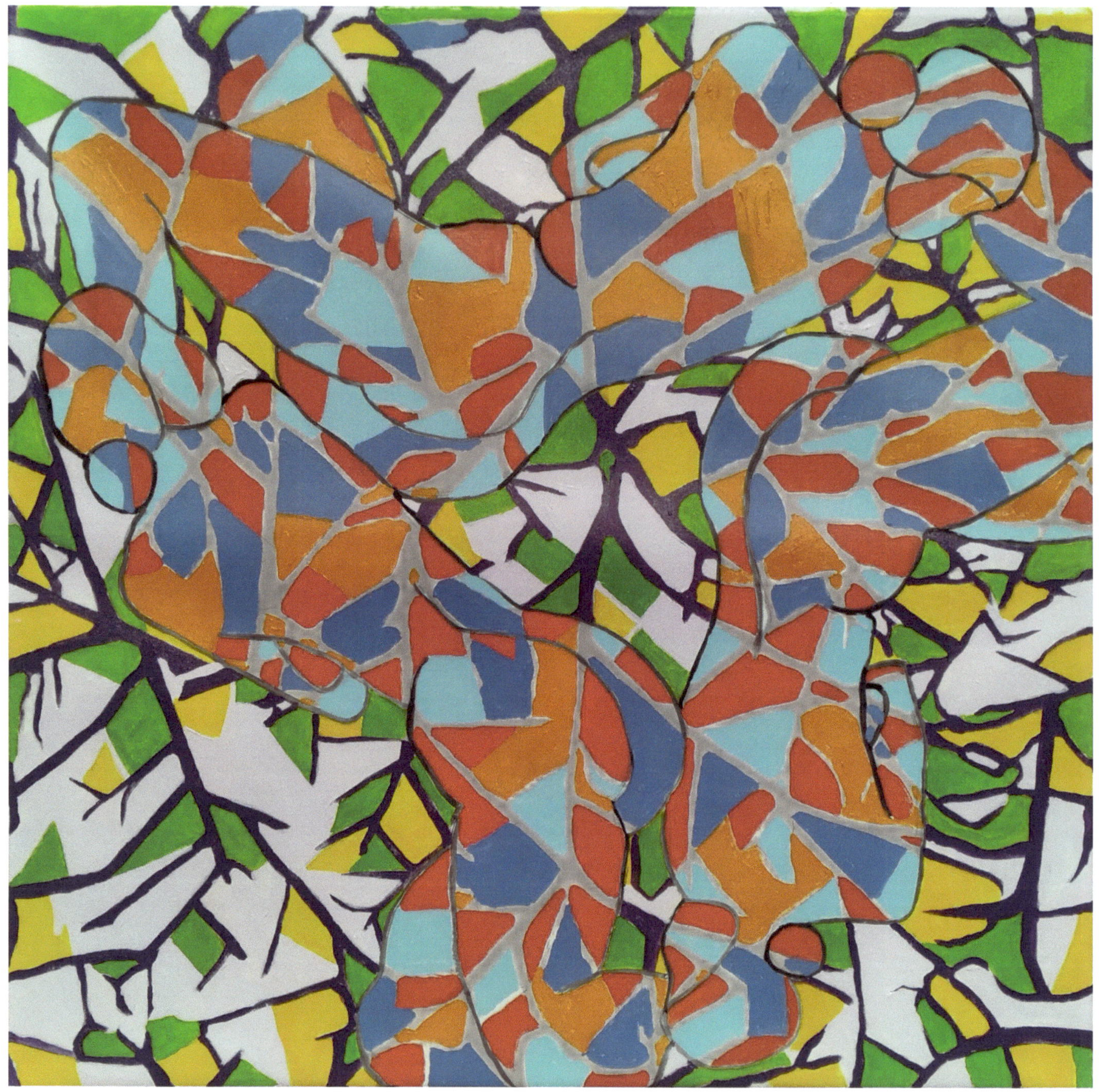

67 Years Old, Tree Women

We had a private garden connected to a big public garden, full of tropical trees and bushes. This is the place we spent most of our time during the pandemic. We often had barbecues there with a small group of friends to enjoy the greenery. It is so interesting to observe the trees and their beautiful proportions. The light coming through the branches, leaves, and flowers gives glimpses of the clouds and sky behind. One day, you should be able to find three Women.

Acrylic on Canvas 36x36 inch

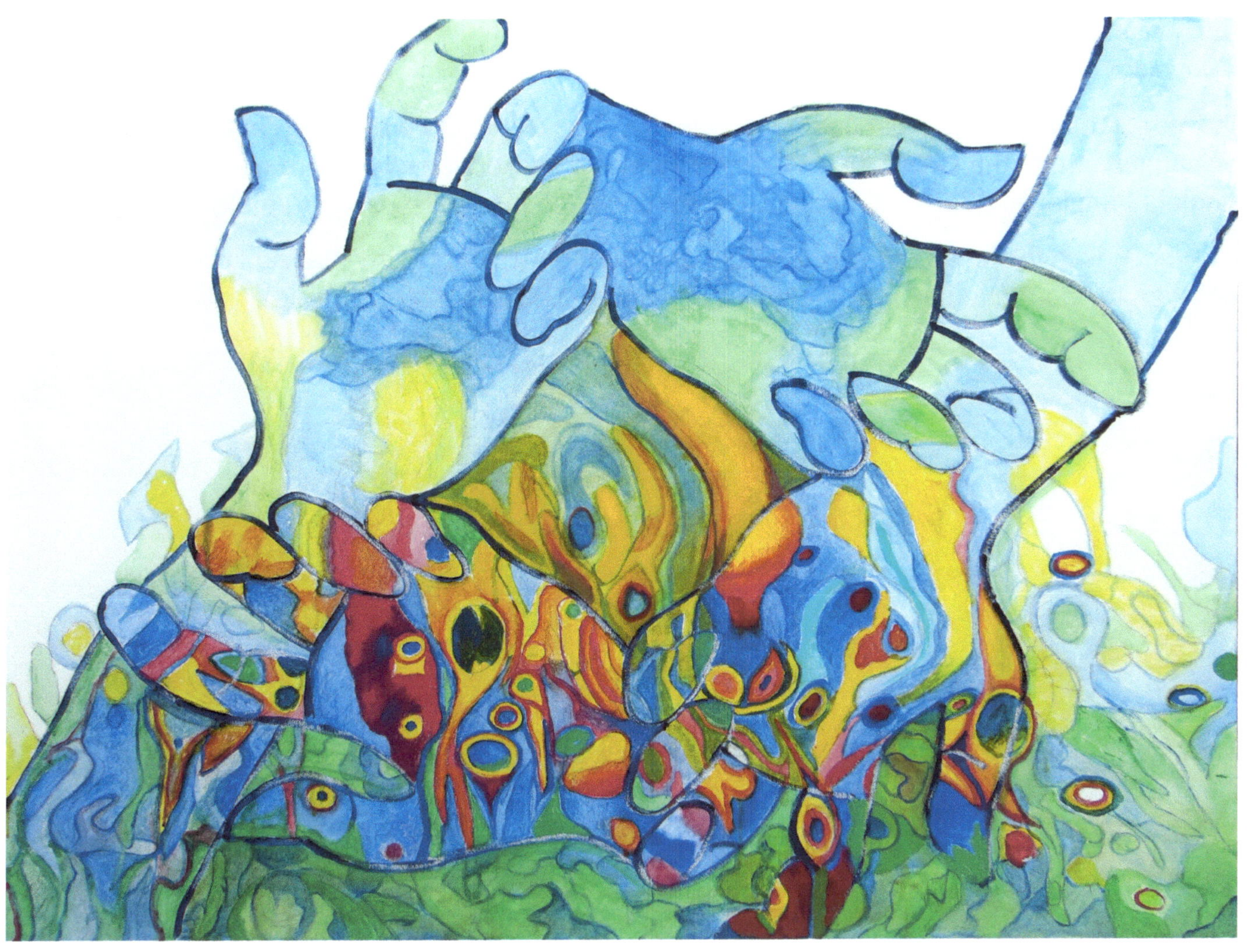

68 Years Old, Mathematical Wonder

I have been working with fractal mathematics since our sail cruising. Aesthetic geometries are found everywhere in nature and the universe. I incorporated fractals in recent paintings, especially the human touch series. The geometries, the beauty, and the forms are woven together to create an image of mathematical harmony. I am flourishing with fractal beauty in my recent paintings. These hands are touched by the fractal-like interference patterns in the soap bubbles. I had seen the beauty of the fractal shapes when I was two years old and they have stayed in my subconscious and are now re-emerging.

Acrylic on Canvas 40x30 inch

Chapter 7 – Future

I am looking forward to the future, my life is back! There are many things I want to do and my art is developing.

I have high hope and confidence for my future years. What they will bring I do not know but I am looking forward to the experience. There will be new challenges, we all are getting older. At the moment I am looking forward, not backwards, into a life that is developing and full of promise.

No Paintings in this chapter...yet. The future will bring more. Join my mailing list on my blog or follow on Instagram to see how the future develops. There is more come……

Biography

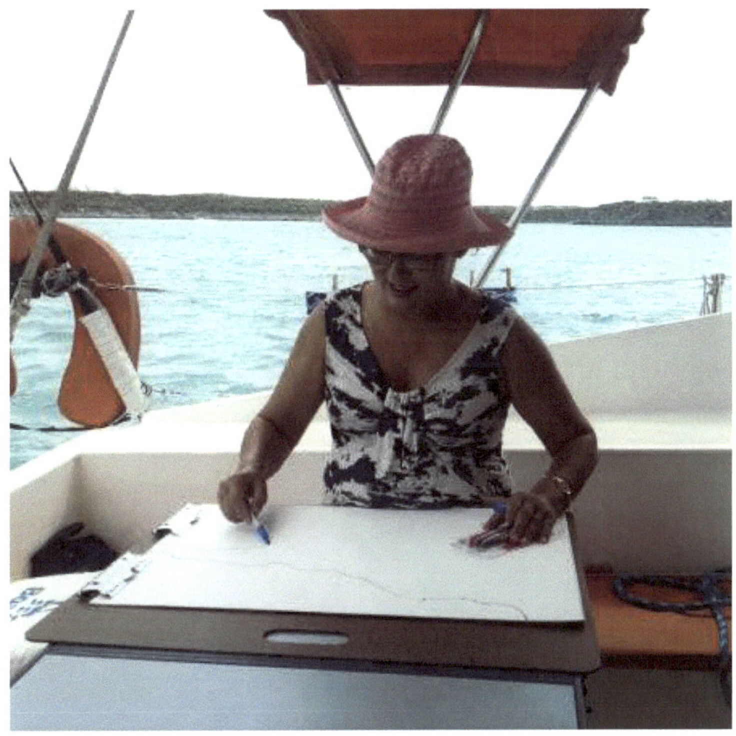

Ms. Lee-Johnson was born in Korea and studied in France, Germany, Korea, and the USA.

She holds a B.F.A in Interior Architecture from the Parsons School of Design and a Major in German literature and language from Ewha Woman's University Seoul. She worked as an Interior Architect in New York City. She further studied at the Art Student League New York, and L'Academie Charpentier in Paris France. She now paints full-time from her Studios in New York City, Puerto Rico, and Italy.

Ms. Lee-Johnson's work celebrates the love of mathematics and nature in a context of cultural differences and abstraction. "It is a magical moment to create the natural look" from inanimate materials.

Ms. Lee-Johnson's art is a clear reflection of intercultural influences provided by her international studies and travel.

In 2005 Ms. Lee-Johnson won The Lloyd Sherward Grant and Award in Abstract Painting. This required her to produce a body of abstract paintings. During this time she started developing her "Abstract Mind" and "My Life" series of psychological impact paintings.

In 2006 Ms. Lee-Johnson won the Merit Scholarship award.

In 2013 Ms. Lee-Johnson won the Dorothy L. Irish Memorial Award for Oil

Painting presented through the National Association of Women Artist in New York.

In 2020 she was shortlisted for LICC award London UK

Ms. Lee-Johnson has exhibited her work in the United States, Europe and Latin America.

Ms. Lee-Johnson is fluent in English, Korean, French and German.

Explanations

My art and this book reference a few concepts that may not be commonly used. This section briefly describes these items. Each could merit a book on its own. More detailed information can be found online by searching for the topic.

Fractals

Fractals are a mathematical concept of self-similar shapes filling a drawing page. One typical example is the Sierpinski Triangle which starts with a triangle and fills it in with smaller triangles each of which is filled in with yet smaller triangles and so on forever.

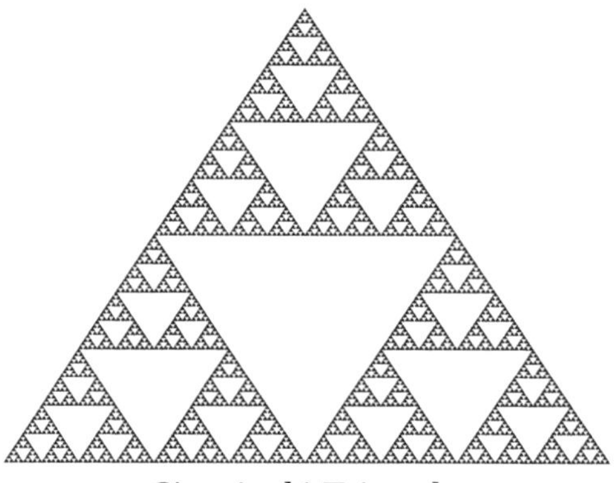

Sierpinski Triangle

In my paintings, I use the term fractal loosely. Clearly, a painting cannot go to smaller scales forever, my brushes are not small enough!

In paintings inspired by sailing on the ocean, I use fractal wavy lines. The wind creates waves on the ocean, big waves have smaller waves on them and the smaller waves have yet smaller waves. This is a typical type of fractal. Complexity and smoothing is added by the boat's movement the boat responds to the different size waves. Being a large object the boat does not move in step with the smaller waves. The big waves move the boat and the smaller waves modify that movement in an apparently random movement. Then my body and hand moves in response to the boat, yet another layer of complexity and smoothing. The final movement of my hand creates the wavy line in the painting. Rough days it is chaotic and violent, calm days it is smooth and flowing. For the mathematically inclined the wavy line in the painting is a sort of integration of the sea state and waves.

In some paintings, I use mathematical fractals, sometimes modified to fit my intention of the feeling in the painting. In other paintings, I use natural fractals such as river deltas or light interference patterns on a soap bubble. In yet others, I use a free-form feeling of a fractal.

Tafoni

Tafoni are cavities naturally formed in rocks. I like them because they are natural and fractal like.

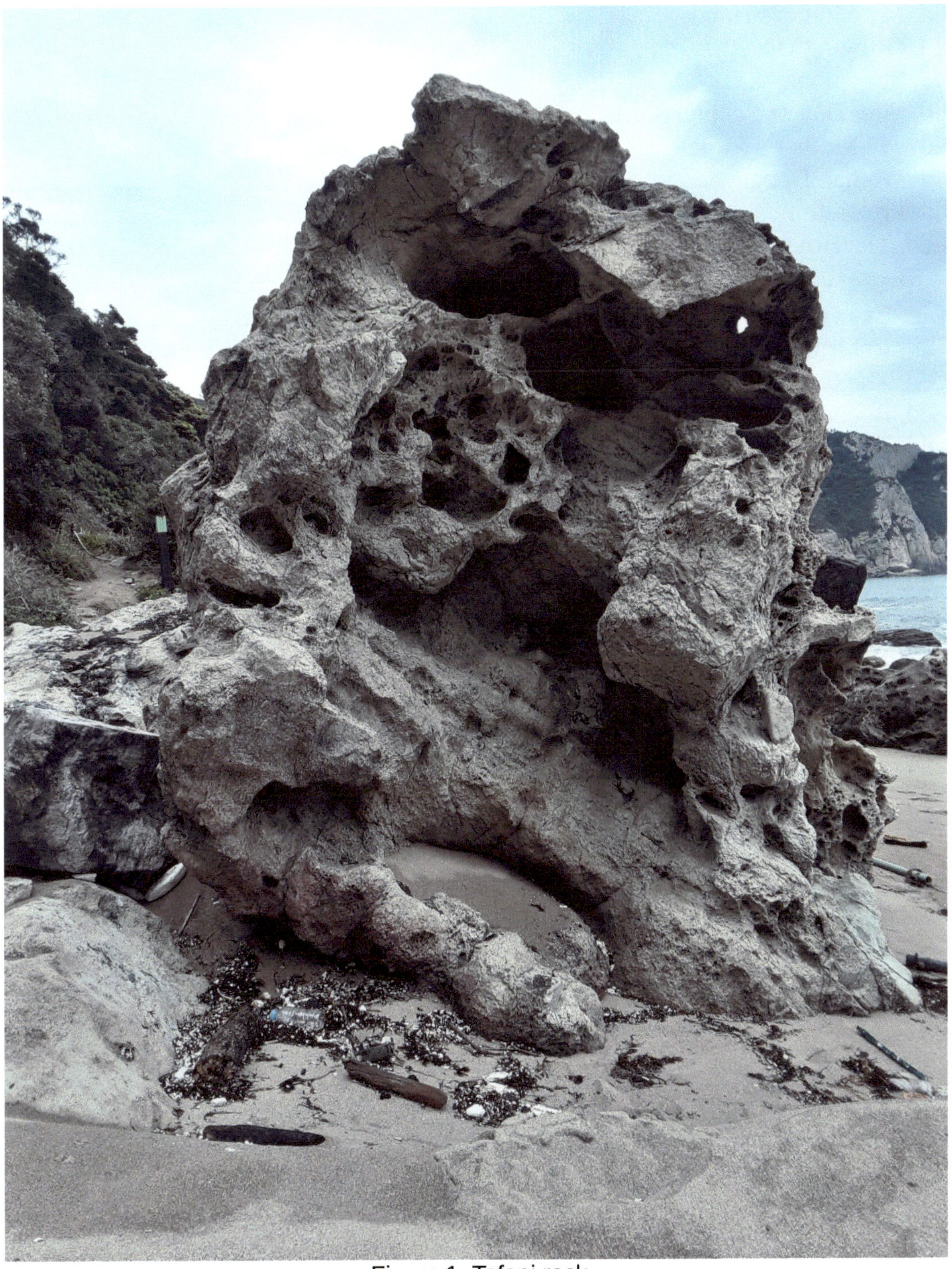

Figure 1: Tafoni rock

Overview Index

www.ingramcontent.com/pod-product-compliance
Ingram Content Group UK Ltd.
Pitfield, Milton Keynes, MK11 3LW, UK
UKHW060120300726
14090UKWH00002B/282

* 9 7 9 8 9 8 8 4 5 6 6 2 9 *